To Tim,
Happy Christmas
love

CW01433299

To Tim,
Happy Christmas
love

Ferrari
TURBO

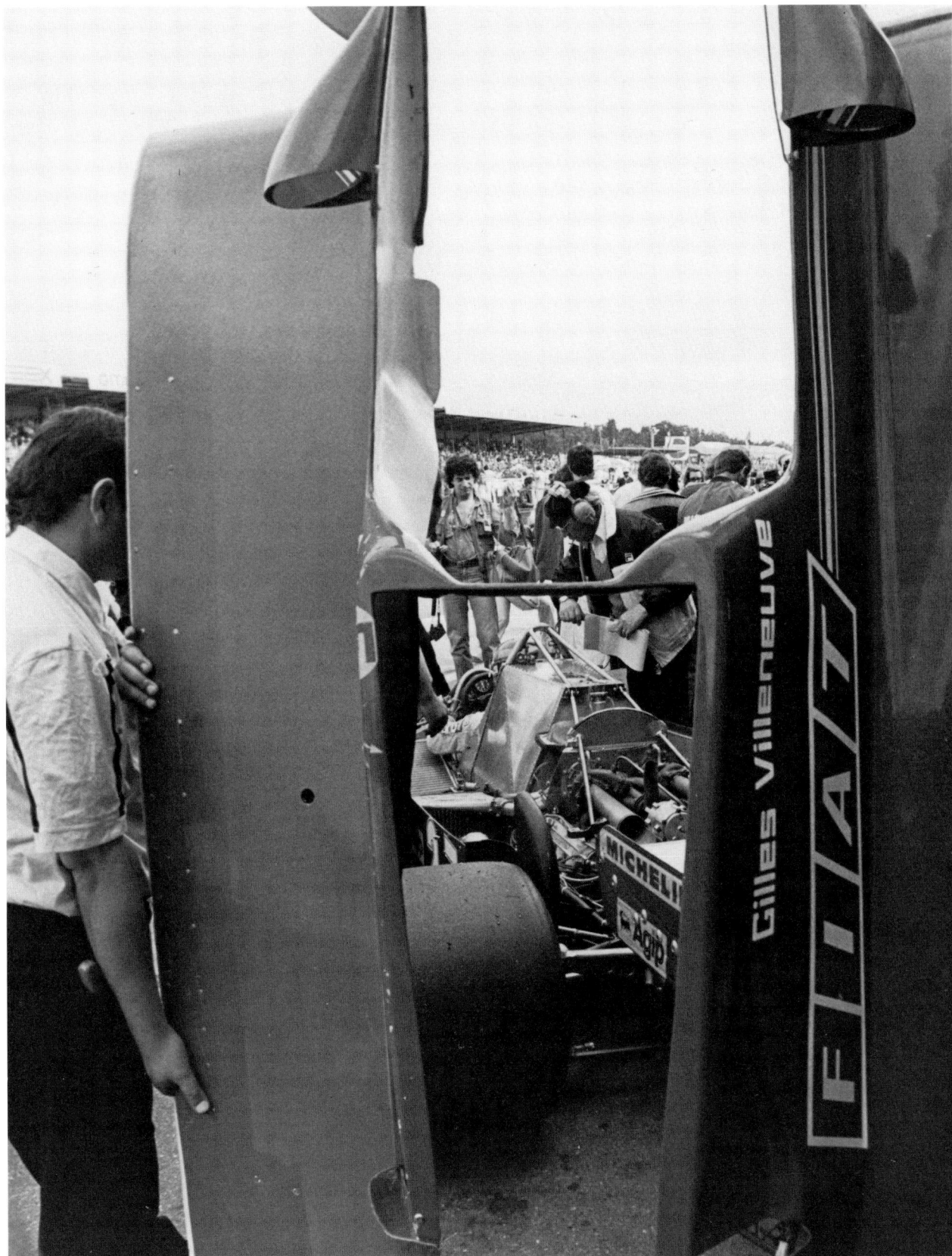

Ferrari
TURBO

Jonathan Thompson

OSPREY

Ferrari
TURBO

In memory of Gilles Villeneuve

Published in 1982 by
Osprey Publishing Limited
12–14 Long Acre
London WC2E 9LP

Member of the George Philip Group

United States distribution by

Motorbooks International
Publishers & Wholesalers Inc.
Osceola, Wisconsin 54020, USA

British Library
Cataloguing in Publication Data
Thompson, Jonathan
Ferrari Turbo
1. Automobile racing—History
2. Ferrari Turbo automobile
I. Title
796.7'2   GV1029.15

ISBN 0-85045-465-4

Editor Tim Parker
Design Jonathan Thompson

Filmset and printed by BAS Printers Limited,
Over Wallop, Hampshire

Contents

Introduction

ITS OTHER EFFICIENCIES ASIDE, an engine produces power in direct proportion to the amount of fuel it burns within a specific period of time. For racing, given a fixed engine capacity, the amount of power produced has been increased by higher engine revolutions; in other words, using the fuel's available energy in a shorter period of time. Most racing engine design has been aimed at improving internal efficiency to permit maximum revolutions reliably for the distance of the racing for which it was conceived. With an established cylinder capacity limit, as exists in Formula 1, all the most advanced techniques of combustion chamber design, valve operation, fuel injection and ignition can only increase the fuel charge by a finite amount.

Because gasoline combustion is dependent upon the amount of air supplied to it in the burning process, it is obvious that increasing the air beyond normal atmospheric supply increases the engine's ability to produce power. By compressing the air within a chamber and either blowing or sucking it through the carburation system, a supercharger increases the air/fuel ratio beyond the outside supply, this ratio being expressed in relation to the existing atmospheric pressure.

It is also obvious that for a given state of supercharger technology, the relative competitiveness of normally aspirated and supercharged racing engines can be adjusted by the capacity limits placed on each type. In the late-1930s, when the highly-developed but still mechanically-driven supercharger was in widespread use, the established relationship for Grand Prix racing was only one-and-a-half to one—that is, 4.5 liters unsupercharged versus 3.0 liters supercharged—and the latter type was absolutely necessary to be competitive. After the Second World War this was changed to a three-to-one equivalency, the supercharged engine capacity being lowered to 1.5 liters, and a competitive relationship was created. Although the supercharged Grand Prix engines still produced 15–20 per cent more power than the best of their 4.5-liter rivals, their use of fuel was significantly greater and even the most efficient pit stops gave away many valuable seconds gained in the earlier laps, while the weight of the fuel the car needed to carry negated some of the power advantage and adversely affected braking and handling. It is a classic story how the 1.5-liter, straight-8, two-stage supercharged Alfa Romeo 158, the dominant Grand Prix car from 1946–1950, was finally overhauled in 1951 by the 4.5-liter unsupercharged Ferrari 375 F1, a relatively simple but efficient car with a single-overhead-camshaft V-12 designed by

Opposite page The Alfa Romeo 158 supercharged straight-eight was the classic Grand Prix car of the late Forties. In the upper photo Achille Varzi poses in the car at the factory in Milano

The great Juan Manuel Fangio won the first of his five World Championships driving an Alfa Romeo 159 in 1951

Aurelio Lampredi. This also brought the existing Formula 1 to an end; although it had two more years to run, there were no existing cars capable of competing with the Ferrari and the 1952–1953 championship events were contested by 2.0-liter Formula 2 cars.

The equivalency was made even less favourable for the supercharged engine in the 1954–1960 Formula 1, permitting 2.5-liter normally aspirated engines and only 750 cc for those with compressors. In addition, racing engine technology had become somewhat less emphasized, as greater attention was given to chassis design, with improvements in roadholding, braking and aerodynamics, the disarmingly simple Cooper-Climax being the great breakthrough to the present rear-engined configuration. Supercharging, always an expensive technique, had fallen into disuse. Various experiments with superchargers were made, but for a quarter of a century, from 1952 until the middle of 1977, every Grand Prix car in World Championship racing had a normally-aspirated engine.

The current Formula 1, established in 1966 and already by far the longest running, has a two-to-one normal to supercharged equivalency (3.0/1.5 litres). Seventeen years ago this was thought to encourage a return to supercharged engines, which were considered ultimately capable of 550–600 bhp, compared to the 350–400 bhp being produced by 3.0-liter unsupercharged engines then. These expectations were later to be proved correct, but for a long time there were no takers.

The turbo-supercharger (now called simply turbocharger in general usage) has been around for much of the twentieth century, its principal use being in high-altitude, piston-engined, propeller-driven aircraft. Put simply, a turbocharger employs the engine's exhaust gases to drive the compressor, with a major improvement in efficiency over a mechanically-driven device. Because of its complexity and expense, its use was confined to military and commercial aircraft during and immediately after the Second World War, and it was some years before the technology was adapted to smaller aircraft for the business and private sectors, diesel trucks and ultimately the automobile.

In 1966 the turbo system was not envisaged for the supercharged 1.5-liter Formula 1 engine, yet within six years, largely through the efforts of Porsche, it had changed the face of Can-Am racing and had started a new era in engine technology for Sport/Prototype and Grand Touring competition. Additionally, with the energy crises that have put pressure (no pun intended) on engine efficiency during the late-1970s and early Eighties, the turbocharger has also been seen as a method for achieving greater (or at least equal) power with reduced fuel consumption in production cars.

Porsche's utter annihilation of the competition (especially the previously dominant McLaren) almost killed the Can-Am series in two years and caused it to be changed to a different format based on single-seat Formula cars. But the German firm's storehouse of turbo expertise led to its application on the smaller engines used in the Prototype and GT categories in long-distance racing, and eventually to an elite series of Porsche Turbos for the road.

The KKK turbochargers used by Porsche were adaptable to any racing engine (although, obviously, for best results a new engine ought to be designed to make the best use of the turbo's characteristics), while other units developed by Garrett AiResearch from its aircraft experience were also available. For Formula 1 the significant turbo project proved to be the adaptation of the 2.0-liter Gordini V-6 engine by Renault for its Prototype programme at Le Mans. Renault had been a pioneer in automobile racing at the beginning of the century, but not until the mid-1970s did the huge French manufacturer re-establish its competition image and strengthen its marketing position to that of Europe's largest producer of passenger cars. Originally raced in unsupercharged form in the 2-liter Sport class in 1973, the Gordini V-6 was subjected to an intensive programme of turbocharger development that ultimately achieved a convincing victory in the French 24-hour event.

Although there had been many rumours about (and now seem to be firm prospects for) the adaptation of Porsche's smallest turbo engine (then 2.1 liters) to the 1.5-liter Formula 1 requirement, it was Renault which made the first move. Lacking experience in current Grand Prix chassis design (in itself a big enough handicap to assume), Renault made an historic turbo debut in the British Grand Prix at Silverstone on 16 July 1977.

At that time Ferrari's 3.0-liter flat-12 engine was on its way to a second World Championship, with two more seasons of competitiveness and another title still in its future, as described in *BOXER*, another Osprey book on racing Ferraris. But the Italian company, always known for advanced engine technology, did not allow Renault's early difficulties with the turbocharger to lull it into complacency. Initial studies for a 1.5-liter turbocharged Ferrari engine began in 1978; once the 120-degree V-6 configuration had been selected, detail design started in 1979. The new car, known as the 126 C (for 120-degree 6, *Compressore*), made its official press debut in June 1980, by which time the team's 3.0-liter boxer-engined 312 T5 was clearly "over the hill".

This book is the story of the 126 C and its first one-and-a-half seasons of competition. It also covers the 1948–1951 supercharged Ferrari Grand Prix cars for historical perspective, and concludes with the turbo conversions of 308 GTB/GTS and Berlinetta Boxer road cars, pointing the way to full factory-engineered, turbo-powered Ferrari production cars in the future.

When this book was nearly finished I was saddened to hear of the death of my friend Peter Coltrin, whose contributions to TURBO and every Ferrari book I've ever worked on have been invaluable. Pete was a great link between the fantastic automotive events of the Emilia region and English-speaking enthusiasts all over the world. Our Man in Modena will never be replaced. I would also like to thank Jeff Hutchinson, who provided the majority of the photographs for this book, as well as Alessandro Stefanini and Bob Tronolone for their absolutely essential cooperation and excellent photography. Additional assistance was given by Sergio Montorsi of Fiat Motors of North America, Tom Kowaleski of Renault USA, Dick Fritz of Ameritech and Bob McClure of BAE. Further acknowledgements appear on page 136.

Norwell, Massachusetts   Jonathan Thompson
June 1982

Chapter 1
the supercharged 125 F1
and 166 Formula Libre

BETWEEN THE 125 F1 of 1948 and the 126 C2 of 1982 there is a continuity of Ferrari Grand Prix cars, each one a thoroughbred owing much to its immediate predecessor and at least something to all the Maranello machinery that went before. No other manufacturer has approached this unbroken thirty-five year line of Formula 1 cars. From Ferrari's 1948 rivals only Alfa Romeo (after a long absence) is still racing today, with Talbot simply a name resurrected for corporate image.

But if the 125 F1 and 126 C2 were put side by side there would be only the red paint and the Prancing Horse emblems on the noses to link them. In contrast to today's low, wide, winged rear-engined machine, with the driver all but submerged at the very front, the 125 F1 was a stubby, narrow, front-engined car, with the driver sitting tall at the back, his arms and torso completely exposed. Even by the standards of the time the 125 F1 was short and high, not nearly as graceful as the Alfa Romeo 158 or Maserati 4CLT, both traditional designs from before the Second World War, or even the big unsupercharged Talbot Lago.

The 125 F1 was the simplest possible *monoposto* (single-seat) chassis in which Ing. Gioacchino Colombo's single-overhead-camshaft 1.5-liter V-12 engine could begin its Grand Prix career. Despite the number of cylinders, the engine itself was a reasonably modest undertaking. As a 1.5-liter sports car unit the V-12 had made its debut in 1947, subsequently being enlarged to 1.9 and then 2 liters for that type of racing. The basic design was a 60-degree vee, with detachable alloy heads on an alloy cylinder block/crankcase, with cast-iron liners shrunk in and held in compression by the heads. The banks were offset 20 mm longitudinally to allow side-by-side forged-steel connecting rods on a seven-main-bearing crankshaft. Each camshaft ran in six bearings, operating the intake and exhaust valves (at an included angle of 60 degrees) in a nearly hemispherical combustion chamber by finger-follower rocker arms and hairpin valve springs.

With the knowledge that the engine would ultimately be supercharged in its high-output form, there were three intake ports per head, with a single 14 mm spark plug at the inner, intake, side of each chamber. The ignition was by twin magnetos, one mounted at the rear of each camshaft. The nitride-hardened crankshaft, turned from a solid steel billet, had throws at 120 degrees, as on an inline six. The bore and stroke were 55×52.5 mm, giving a single-cylinder capacity of 124.73 cm^3 (hence the 125 designation) and a total of 1496.77 cm^3.

As a touring car engine with a single Weber 30 DCF carburetor and a

Nino Farina tests the first Ferrari 125 F1 at Torino in August 1948

The original car, now painted, was one of Ferrari's three entries in the Italian Grand Prix, driven by Prince Bira

Farina crashes his 125 F1 into the haybales in the rainy Grand Prix

11

compression ratio of 8.0:1, the 1.5-liter V-12 produced a mere 72 bhp at 5600 rpm. For sports car events, with three Webers, a compression ratio of 8.5:1 and other modifications, the output was 100 bhp at 7000 rpm. With the compression ratio reduced to 6.5:1 and a single-stage Roots-type supercharger sucking through a Weber 40 DO3C carburetor, Colombo's engine was still a modest debutant in Grand Prix racing, producing only 230 bhp at 7000 rpm. In comparison, the eight-cylinder inline, two-stage supercharged Alfa Romeo 158 was producing 275 bhp at 7500 rpm on a boost of 3.55 pounds/square inch at that time (raised to 350 bhp by 1950 and an ultimate 425 bhp on the Tipo 159 with a 4.27-psi boost in 1951). Even the four-cylinder Maserati 4CLT/48 (San Remo) engine produced 260 bhp at 7000 rpm.

The Grand Prix Ferrari engine's initially disappointing power output called for the lightest possible chassis, this being the main reason for the extremely short wheelbase of 2160 mm (85.1 inches). The frame was a simple ladder type with oval-section longitudinal main members and the suspension followed early Ferrari practice, with transverse leaf springing in front and swing axles located by single radius arms at the back. The power was transmitted by a five-speed gearbox mounted behind the engine. As with all Grand Prix cars of the period, the brakes were large-diameter finned drums and the wheels were Borrani (Rudge-type) wire knock-offs. The aluminium bodywork, built over a light tubular superstructure, was blunt and uninspired but had the good proportions always associated with Italian *carrozzeria*.

Because of Ferrari's belief in robust construction, the extreme simplicity—one could almost say crudeness—of the design did not result in an especially light car, the dry weight of 700 kilograms (1543 pounds) being only marginally lower than the Alfa Romeo's and 150 kg greater than the Maserati's. Even taking into account the higher fuel consumption of the two latter machines requiring greater tankage or longer pit stops, the first Grand Prix Ferrari was not a competitive machine, at least on paper.

Ferrari took the original, still unpainted 125 F1 to Valentino Park in Torino in August 1948 for its initial testing in preparation for the Italian Grand Prix to be held on that circuit on 5 September. Giuseppe Farina (later to become the first World Champion in 1950, with Alfa Romeo) was the driver. Although the short wheelbase did nothing for the high-speed stability, there were no major problems during the outing.

If Ferrari's machinery was modest in concept, his abilities as a team organizer and as a prolific producer of chassis were emphasized by the appearance of no less than three neatly-prepared 125 F1 *monoposti* at the race in September. Two new chassis, with similar bodywork but more handsome noses, were presented for Farina (number 26) and Raymond Sommer (28), while the original car (68) was given to Prince Bira. None could match the speed of the Alfa Romeos—Jean-Pierre Wimille's 158 won the event—but Sommer had a furious duel in the rain with the Maserati of Luigi Villoresi, who finally took second place a few lengths ahead of the Ferrari. Farina crashed into a straw bale when running fourth and Bira dropped out when his gearbox failed, so Ferrari's Grand Prix debut was marked by the full range of fortunes. the main fault being transmission failure.

Although Farina won a minor event against limited opposition at

13

Opposite page *The original 125 F1 had a single-stage supercharged, single-overhead-camshaft, 1.5-liter engine*

Villoresi finished second to Ascari in the 1949 Swiss Grand Prix at Bern

15

Mechanics change the twelve spark plugs of Peter Whitehead's privately-entered 125 F1 before the 1949 Swiss event

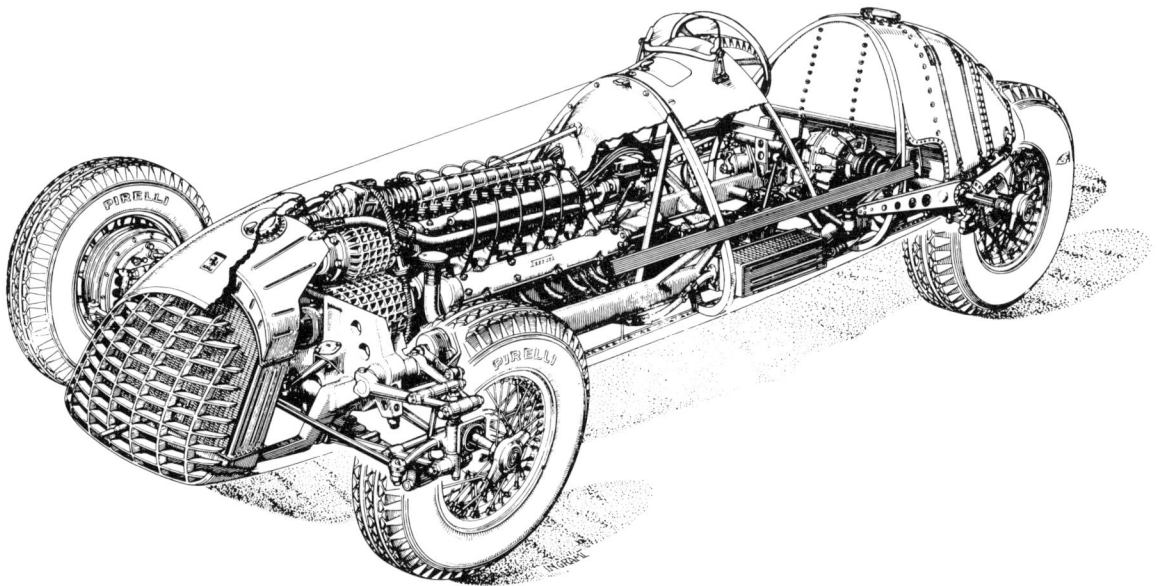

La **Ferrari** vincitrice del Gran Premio d'Europa a Monza

Garda on 24 October (Ferrari's first Grand Prix victory with a car bearing his name), the 125 F1 in its original form was little more than a narrower, blown version of the sports car and could not be expected to produce the major victories Ferrari sought. All of the cars failed to finish in two more Grands Prix at Monza and Barcelona with transmission failure, the one weak point in the otherwise sturdy design.

After losing all of its leading drivers in separate tragedies, Alfa Romeo decided not to compete in 1949. This left the way clear for Ferrari to have a direct battle with Maserati (and to a lesser extent, Talbot). Villoresi and his protegé Alberto Ascari were hired to drive for the Scuderia that season; despite their skill, especially the brilliance of the younger Italian, the team was under no illusion that the 125 F1 was a long-term winner. With its mediocre high-speed handling and moderate power it was barely a match for its current opposition and had little chance of withstanding the later appearance of any high-powered rivals. So while the two team drivers, and Englishman Peter Whitehead in a privately-entered 125 F1, contested the European events of early 1949, Ferrari instructed Colombo to produce an almost entirely new 125 F1 that would eliminate its shortcomings.

While Colombo and the Ferrari technical staff labored into the summer on the new car, Villoresi and Ascari made effective use of the existing machines, the former winning at Zandvoort in Holland and the latter at Bern in Switzerland and at Silverstone in England on 20 August. Silverstone was the first run for the works team in Great Britain and was convincing; with Villoresi also taking third place.

The much revised engine had the same dimensions but with its twin-overhead-camshaft cylinder heads and two-stage supercharger it was in effect an all-new design. (One of the characteristics of Ferrari engine design has been the strong bottom end that can hold up under ever-greater top-end development.) The four camshafts, the first such system on a Ferrari but one that in later years has become almost a trademark, were gear-driven. The carburetor was a Weber 50 WCF and the compression ratio 7.0:1. In initial tests the engine produced a satisfying 290 bhp at 7500 rpm, this being raised to 315 in 1950.

No startling innovations were made in the chassis, but handling was vastly improved by the longer wheelbase, now 2380 cm (93.7 inches), and the bodywork, benefiting from the extra length, was more streamlined if no lower. Altogether it was a completely transformed 125 F1 that made its debut at Monza for the European Grand Prix on 11 September, 1949. Two of the new two-stage, four-cam cars were entered for Villoresi and Ascari, while older machines were fielded for Sommer and Felice Bonetto and the private entry of Whitehead also appeared. Ascari had no trouble dominating the event and Villoresi ran second until his gearbox failed. It was obvious that the still-young Ferrari factory had entered a new phase with the appearance of this second-generation 125 F1, but it was also significant that the speed was inferior to that achieved by Alfa Romeo the previous year.

As with the sports car engines, the single-stage 125 F1 unit had already been enlarged to 2 liters and run without supercharging in Formula B and Formula 2 events. At that time there was little distinction made between the 166 Spyder Corsa sports cars, running without fenders and lights, and the true 166 F2 *monoposti*, although the

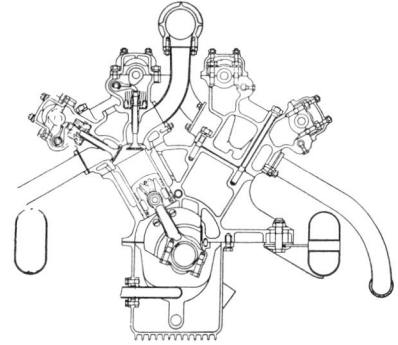

Although using a similar bottom end, the twin-overhead-camshaft version of the 125 F1 developed by Ing. Colombo in 1949 was essentially an all-new unit

Opposite page, top *British debut for Scuderia Ferrari was at Silverstone in 1949. Ascari's 125 F1 (number 8, in the background) was the winner*

Opposite page, bottom *Factory cutaway drawing shows the details of the long-wheelbase, two-stage supercharged 125 F1 developed in the summer of 1949*

17

Gioacchino Colombo with his two-stage 125 F1 in the Ferrari engine test room

Superchargers were mounted at front, ignition at rear on 125 F1. Frame was a simple ladder design with oval tubing

18

Unfinished aluminum body for first four-cam 125 F1 sits on stands at Maranello. Longer wheelbase improved body lines

Alberto Ascari takes still-unpainted two-stage 125 F1 out for first run at Monza

Enzo Ferrari discusses car's prospects after its initial laps. Designer Colombo listens from the back (at far left)

19

Ascari after winning the two-stage car's debut race, the 1949 Italian Grand Prix at Monza. Ferrari led the entire event, but the Alfa Romeo team was absent

latter were of course more competitive. Longer-wheelbase versions of the 166 F2 were built for 1950 and eventually the type benefited from the latest De Dion rear suspension and lower bodywork, but more important to our story were the blown 166 Formula Libre cars.

Three cars of this type, long-wheelbase Monza-type chassis with engines of 60 × 58.8 mm and 1995 cm³, were taken to Argentina in December 1949 for a series of four Formula Libre events that extended into January 1950, the middle of the Argentine summer. Driven by Villoresi, Ascari and Juan Manuel Fangio, the cars produced approximately 350 bhp and had no trouble with the minimal opposition, mainly Maserati 4CLTs with 1720 cm³ engines. Ascari won the Peron Cup and the Mar del Plata Grand Prix, and Villoresi the Eva Peron Cup and Rosario Grand Prix. Fangio, the great Argentine ace who would become World Champion five times during the Fifties, was competitive with the Italian pair, leading them at Mar del Plata, but he had a series of incidents and his best finish was second in the Peron Cup. Older chassis with 2-liter engines were driven in the series by Farina, Dorino Serafini (a Ferrari test driver) and Benedicto Campos, each enjoying one second place finish.

With the reappearance of the Alfa Romeo 158 for the 1950 European season it became immediately apparent that the latest 1.5-liter two-stage Ferrari 125 F1 was still no match for it. Contesting the first World Championship with 350-bhp engines and a driving team consisting of Farina, Fangio and Luigi Fagioli (the famous Fa-Fa-Fa trio), Alfa Romeo dominated the season, winning all six of the championship events. Despite the gradual improvement of the 125 F1 chassis, including De Dion rear suspension, Ferrari had to be content with the lower placings.

But Ferrari, never content to pursue a single avenue of technology, had already given Colombo's assistant Aurelio Lampredi the go-ahead to produce a completely new series of V-12s. Making their debut in 3.3-liter sports car form as the 275 S in the 1950 Mille Miglia, these new large-displacement engines were quickly adapted for Formula 1 use when it was realized that the lower fuel consumption of the big unsupercharged engines could make them more than a match for the 1.5-liter blown units, which required a heavier fuel load and at least one pit stop in a Grand Prix. The 3.3-liter unsupercharged 275 F1 made its debut at Spa-Francorchamps, Belgium in June and it was joined by a 4.1-liter 340 F1 at Geneva, Switzerland in July. All development on the 125 F1 ceased. For the Italian Grand Prix at Monza on 3 September, the full 4.5-liter 375 F1 made its debut and the first series of supercharged Ferrari Grand Prix cars came to an end. The 166 Formula Libre cars were entered privately in the South American races of 1951 and 1952; Froilan Gonzalez scored his famous victories over the Mercedes-Benz team the former year, and the last race for the type was Fangio's victory in the Buenos Aires City Grand Prix on 9 March, 1952.

While Alfa Romeo Tipo 159, stretching the pre-war design to the limit, was successful in winning yet another World Championship in 1951, the supercharged era itself was ending. More than twenty years would go by before turbocharging would be adapted to road racing and a quarter of a century elapsed between the last race of a supercharged Grand Prix car and the debut of Renault's turbocharged Formula 1 car at Silverstone on 16 July, 1977.

Opposite page *1950 Monte Carlo photos give good comparison between older single-stage 125 F1 (Sommer's light blue car,* top) *and latest works two-stage, long-wheelbase machine of Villoresi*

22

The Alfa Romeo team again dominated Grand Prix racing in 1950. Fangio (14), Farina (16) and Fagioli make up the front row at Bern, with Ferraris of Villoresi (22, with De Dion rear suspension) and Ascari (18, swing axles) in second row

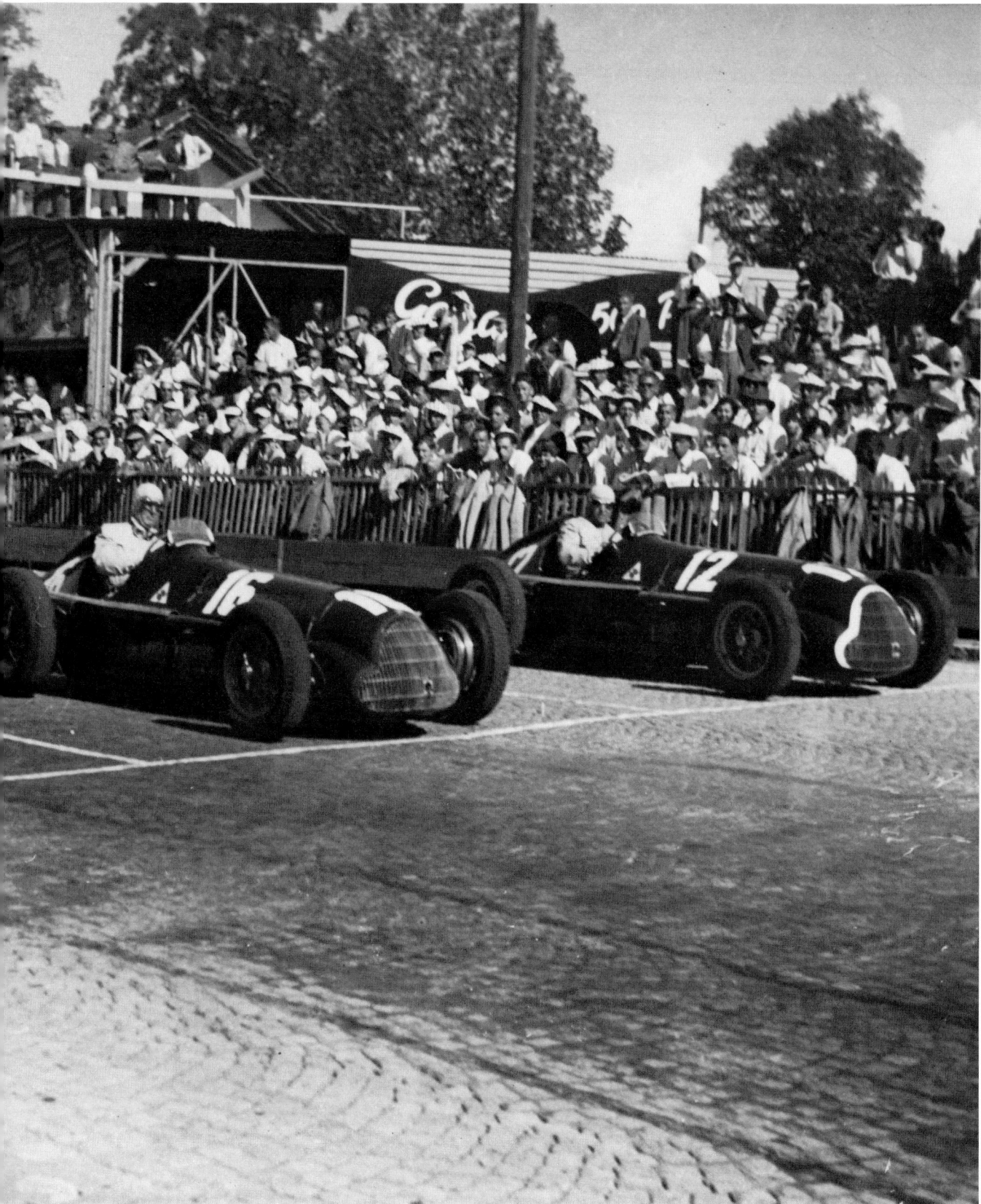

Start at Spa-Francorchamps, with 125 F1 of Villoresi between the leading Alfas and new unsupercharged 275 F1 of Ascari further back, ahead of the Talbots

Tadini in an older single-stage 125 F1 in the 1950 Grand Prix des Nations

24

Peter Whitehead in his 125 F1, before the start of 1950 Palermo race in Argentina

Opposite page, top Fangio leads Ascari and Villoresi at Mar del Plata in 1950. All three drove 2-liter 166 Formula Libre versions of long-wheelbase two-stage car. Below, Froilan Gonzalez demonstrates his arms-out style at Buenos Aires in 1951; he defeated Mercedes-Benz team in older short-wheelbase 166 F2

Performances, 1948 through March 1952

Date	Circuit	Driver	Chassis	Result
5 September 1948	Torino (I)	Sommer	125 F1(s)	3rd
		Farina	125 F1(s)	R, accident
		Bira	125 F1(s)	R, transmission
17 October 1948	Monza (I)	Sommer	125 F1(s)	R, driver
		Farina	125 F1(s)	R, transmission
24 October 1948	Garda (I)	Farina	125 F1(s)	1st
31 October 1948	Barcelona (E)	Farina	125 F1(s)	R, transmission
		Bira	125 F1(s)	R, transmission
		Pola	125 F1(s)	R, engine
13 February 1949	Rosario (RA)	Farina	125 F1(s)	1st
27 March 1949	Gavea (BR)	Farina	125 F1(s)	2nd
3 April 1949	San Remo (I)	Whitehead	125 F1(s)	R, engine
28 April 1949	Jersey (GB)	Whitehead	125 F1(s)	7th
14 May 1949	Silverstone (GB)	Whitehead/ Folland	125 F1(s)	8th
		Mays/ Richardson	125 F1(T)	R, accident
19 June 1949	Spa-Francorchamps (B)	Villoresi	125 F1(s)	2nd
		Ascari	125 F1(s)	3rd
		Whitehead	125 F1(s)	4th
3 July 1949	Bern (CH)	Ascari	125 F1(s)	1st
		Villoresi	125 F1(s)	2nd
		Whitehead	125 F1(s)	9th
17 July 1949	Reims (F)	Whitehead	125 F1(s)	3rd
		Villoresi	125 F1(s)	R, brakes
31 July 1949	Zandvoort (NL)	Villoresi	125 F1(s)	1st
		Ascari	125 F1(s)	R, suspension
		Whitehead	125 F1(s)	R, ignition
20 August 1949	Silverstone (GB)	Ascari	125 F1(s)	1st
		Villoresi	125 F1(s)	3rd
		Whitehead	125 F1(s)	R, accident
28 August 1949	Lausanne (CH)	Ascari	125 F1(s)	2nd
		Whitehead	125 F1(s)	10th
		Villoresi	125 F1(s)	R, transmission
11 September 1949	Monza (I)	Ascari	125 F1(t)	1st
		Sommer	125 F1(s)	5th
		Villoresi	125 F1(t)	R, transmission
		Bonetto	125 F1(s)	R, final drive
		Whitehead	125 F1(s)	R, ignition
25 September 1949	Brno (CZ)	Whitehead	125 F1(s)	1st

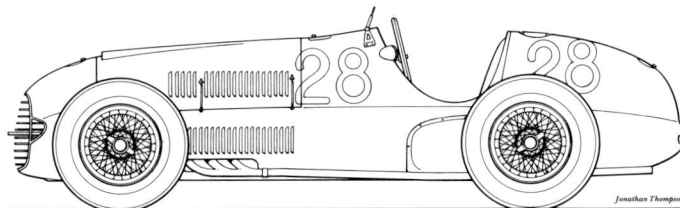

1948 short-wheelbase, single-stage 125 F1 as driven by Raymond Sommer at Torino

Date	Circuit	Driver	Chassis	Result
18 December 1949	Palermo (RA)	Ascari	166 FL(t)	1st
		Fangio	166 FL(t)	2nd
		Villoresi	166 FL(t)	3rd
		Campos	166 FL(s)	4th
8 January 1950	Palermo (RA)	Villoresi	166 FL(t)	1st
		Serafini	166 FL(s)	2nd
		Fangio	166 FL(t)	4th
		Ascari	166 FL(t)	R, accident
15 January 1950	Mar del Plata (RA)	Ascari	166 FL(t)	1st
		Farina	166 FL(s)	2nd
		Fangio	166 FL(t)	R, accident
		Villoresi	166 FL(t)	R, accident
22 January 1950	Rosario (RA)	Villoresi	166 FL(t)	1st
		Campos	166 FL(s)	2nd
		Farina	166 FL(s)	3rd
		Ascari	166 FL(t)	R, overheating
		Fangio	166 FL(t)	R, ignition
10 April 1950	Pau (F)	Villoresi	125 F1(t)	2nd
		Sommer	125 F1(s)	4th
16 April 1950	San Remo (I)	Villoresi	125 F1(t)	2nd
		Vallone	125 F1(s)	4th
		Ascari	125 F1(t)	R, engine
		Serafini	125 F1(s)	R, ignition
		Sommer	125 F1(s)	R, transmission
		Whitehead	125 F1(s)	R, ignition
21 May 1980	Monte Carlo (MC)	Ascari	125 F1(t)	2nd
		Sommer	125 F1(s)	4th
		Villoresi	125 F1(t)	R, axle
4 June 1950	Bern (CH)	Ascari	125 F1(t)	R, lubrication
		Villoresi	125 F1(t)	R, engine
18 June 1950	Spa-Francorchamps	Villoresi	125 F1(t)	6th
2 July 1950	Reims (F)	Whitehead	125 F1(s)	3rd
13 July 1950	Jersey (GB)	Whitehead	125 F1(s)	1st
23 July 1950	Zandvoort (NL)	Villoresi	125 F1(t)	2nd
		Whitehead	125 F1(s)	4th
12 August 1950	Dundrod (IRL)	Whitehead	125 F1(s)	1st
26 August 1950	Silverstone (GB)	Whitehead	125 F1(s)	3rd
		Ascari	125 F1(T)	R, accident
3 September 1950	Monza (I)	Whitehead	125 F1(s)	7th
18 February 1951	Costanera (RA)	Gonzalez	166 FL(s)	1st
		Galvez	166 FL(s)	4th
25 February 1951	Costanera (RA)	Gonzalez	166 FL(s)	1st
20 January 1952	Gavea (BR)	Gonzalez	166 FL(s)	1st
		Landi	166 FL(s)	2nd
9 March 1952	Buenos Aires (RA)	Fangio	166 FL(t)	1st
		Gonzalez	166 FL(s)	2nd
		Landi	166 FL(s)	3rd

Key: (s) Single-stage short chassis;
(t) Two-stage long chassis;
(T) Thinwall Special.

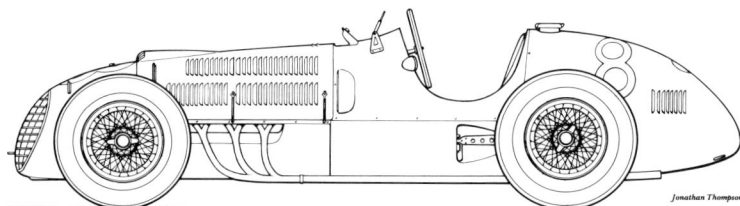

Jonathan Thompson

1949 long-wheelbase, two-stage 125 F1
as driven by Alberto Ascari at Monza.
(Both drawings to 1/40 scale)

Chapter 2
the turbocharged Formula 1 Renault

ALTHOUGH ITS RACING HERITAGE goes back to the turn of the century, the great French automobile manufactuer Régie Renault did not have recent Formula 1 experience to draw upon when it embarked upon its amibitious turbo program in 1975. This was to some extent offset by the development of a series of sports/racing cars, also turbocharged, which gave the firm a step-by-step program to advance its knowledge of modern racing car technology while pursuing an outright victory in the Le Mans 24-hour event. It was only when this victory was achieved, by Didier Pironi and Jean-Pierre Jaussaud in a Renault Alpine A 442B in 1978, that the company gave its full-time attention to Formula 1.

The Formula 1 project (as well as the Le Mans cars) had its origins in the Alpine A 440 sports/racing car of 1973. Its engine was a 2-liter Gordini-designed 90-degree V-6, producing a very substantial 295 bhp at 10,400 rpm; this unit provided the basis for all subsequent Renault racing engines (discounting the rally cars, of course).

The American Garrett AiResearch company had produced turbochargers for aircraft and trucks before its technology was adapted to Indianapolis racing engines. When the French Elf fuel company gave Renault its backing to pursue a lengthy, difficult and expensive program of Formula 1 turbo development in February 1975, the Garrett system was used as a basis. The original 2-liter Gordini engine had a bore and stroke of 86×57.3 mm; to reduce the capacity to the 1.5-liter limit established for turbocharged engines in Formula 1, the stroke was shortened to 42.8 mm. This extremely oversquare ratio of bore to stroke resulted in a total displacement of 1492 cm³. On the early examples of the engine, with high combustion-chamber temperatures and piston failures to deal with, the output was in excess of 450 bhp, less than the best 3-liter Formula 1 units were producing at the time but a promising beginning. Throttle-lag, a characteristic of the turbo engine in which the power applied by the driver does not come into play until some fractions of a second later, was a major problem; not only did it prevent the engine's full power from being employed immediately when exiting from corners, it created a difficult task for the driver, who had to learn a technique of judging power needs in advance. The throttle-lag was to a large extent eliminated by the later use of the twin-turbo system; also, by that time the drivers had become so used to this turbo characteristic that they were no longer consciously affected by it. In early 1977 an engine developing 510 bhp at 11,000 rpm on a compression ratio of 6.8:1 was considered sufficiently

First Formula 1 Renault turbo was tested in this Prototype Laboratoire *in 1976*

Original F1 turbo configuration was like that of Sport/Prototypes, with single turbine at back. Gordini V6 was a 90-degree engine displacing 1492 cc.

29

1978 Renault victory at Le Mans, by Didier Pironi and Jean-Pierre Jaussaud, allowed firm to change main effort to F1

reliable to justify a program of several Grand Prix events that season.

Renault had also been involved in Formula 2, and the first test chassis for the Formula 1 engine, the *Prototype Laboratoire* announced in late 1976, was based on that experience. It was a relatively simple design with a wide monocoque (this was before the days of ground-effect chassis) and the conventional suspension of inboard front springs operated by wishbones, and outboard rear springs working with upper and lower links and parallel radius arms. The gearbox was a Hewland of the type employed by most of the teams running Ford-Cosworth V-8s.

The first RS 01 chassis was tested in May 1977 by Jean-Pierre Jabouille at the Paul Ricard circuit. A veteran driver but one limited in Formula 1 experience, Jabouille proved to be the ideal man for the Renault cockpit; he was adaptable to the peculiar demands of the turbo engine and he grew in competitive experience as the car became more and more raceworthy. As tested at Ricard, the RS 01 showed great aerodynamic refinement over the *Prototype Laboratoire*; the front had a full-width nose of the type pioneered by Tyrrell, the engine had a streamlined cover and the rear wing was a biplane arrangement with deep endplates.

For the car's racing debut at Silverstone on 16 July the nose was changed for a narrower one with separate planes on each side, and the heat generated by the turbo made it necessary to discard the engine cover. The team, managed by Jean Sage, had no expectation of immediate competitiveness but it was hoped that RS 01-1 would make a promising debut. In fact, Jabouille qualified only twenty-first on the grid and was forced to retire with a turbo failure after only sixteen laps. The Grand Prix establishment did not feel threatened. At that time Niki Lauda was turning in a series of consistent performances with the Ferrari 312 T2 that would lead to his second championship. Renault gave the next two Grand Prix a miss while it concentrated on the turbo problems, returning for the last two races on the European calendar and the two North American events. Although RS 01-1 qualified a decent tenth fastest at Zandvoort, it retired in three successive races and failed to qualify for the Canadian Grand Prix at Mosport.

Nevertheless, Renault and Elf were prepared for a long development period. Two additional chassis were built for 1978, RS 01-2 and 3, and the original car did not appear again. Jabouille was still the team's only driver, although he now had two chassis to choose from and, after Le Mans in June, the entire resources of the Renault competition department behind him. The first finish was recorded at Monte Carlo in May (tenth) and the first championship points (3) were gained by Jabouille's fourth-place finish in the Watkins Glen race in October. His highest qualifying position had been third, gained at both the Osterreichring and Monza circuits where the turbo's high maximum speed came into full effect. During the season the Renault's reliability record was not good, with only five finishes out of fourteen starts; all of the retirements (except a gearbox failure in Austria) were because of turbocharger or piston failures. These were the direct result of the high combustion-chamber temperatures; the cure was an intercooler developed by Renault technical director Francois Castaing. This lowered air intake temperature significantly at some expense in added weight but also gave more power.

Jean-Pierre Jabouille tests RS 01 at Paul Ricard circuit in May 1977 (opposite page, top); note full engine cover. Below, the debut of the same car in the British Grand Prix at Silverstone in July, with different front wing and without engine cover

31

Leading Grand Prix contender at time of Renault turbo debut was Niki Lauda, who won 1977 championship with Ferrari 312 T2, a 3-liter car with flat-12 engine

Jabouille in RS 01 at Monte Carlo in 1978; turbo did not finish in the points until Watkins Glen race later that year

33

Leading Grand Prix car of 1978 was the Lotus (JPS) 79, which made ground-effect chassis breakthrough; Mario Andretti was the World Champion

34

For the throttle-lag problem the twin-turbo system was first tested at Dijon in April 1979; this called for a second intercooler and it was difficult incorporating all the additional plumbing while not disturbing the airflow through the sidepods or over the rear wing. (By that time the ground-effect system introduced by Lotus was an absolute necessity for any competitive Formula 1 car.) A fourth RS 01 was added but an entirely new chassis, designated RS10, was under development for a debut in Spain at the end of April. Originally designated RS 10-01, 02 and 03, this series incorporated the ground-effect solutions that had been introduced as modifications on the earlier cars; it would eventually consist of four chassis with the revised numbering system RS 10, 11, 12 and 14. The extremely capable René Arnoux, whose Formula 1 career had been on the point of extinction because of the inferior equipment with which he had had to cope, made a big step up when he was chosen to join Jabouille on the Renault team.

The older chassis RS 01-2 enjoyed the distinction of being the first Renault—and, of course, the first turbo—to start a Formula 1 race from the pole, this having occured on the high-altitude circuit at Kyalami in South Africa on 3 March. Jabouille led for one lap but was forced to let the Ferrari 312 T4s of Gilles Villeneuve and Jody Scheckter go by; he retired after forty-seven laps with a valve-spring failure. The great day that Renault had been working toward came on 1 July, appropriately in the French Grand Prix at Dijon. Jabouille and Arnoux qualified RS 11 and 12 in the two top grid positions and finished first and third in the race after a battle with Villeneuve, who led for forty-six of the eighty laps. Arnoux set the fastest lap and was only narrowly beaten for second place by the tenacious performance of the Canadian.

From that point on the Renault turbo was the car to beat in sheer speed. It was generally good for pole position even if the turbo reliability was still poor and kept it from finishing most of the time. Arnoux scored two second places and a sixth in addition to the third he had taken at Dijon; this made him eighth in the final 1979 World Championship standings, while Jabouille was thirteenth, the nine points he scored from his Dijon victory being the only ones he got all year. In fact, he only finished on two other occasions, an eighth at Monte Carlo and a tenth at Interlagos. This was the story of the turbo Formula 1 car so far: blindingly fast on the circuits which suited it but woefully fragile over full race distance. Still, great progress had been made each year and the Renault turbo was now taken seriously by the rival teams. Those with an eye to the future, notably Ferrari, had already begun turbo programs of their own.

For 1980 Renault had its third-generation chassis, the 20 series which would comprise eight machines in all: RE 20, 21, 22, 23, 24 and 25, and later the RE 26 and 27 in 'B' configuration. The first four 20-series were converted from RS 10–14. In the past the RS designation had indicated Renault Sport; the new one stood for Renault Elf. The 20 series was lighter and had new sidepods and revised skirts, while the engine had new valve springs and greater reliability was claimed. It was interesting that the factory press handouts gave a figure of only 500 bhp at 11,000 rpm; while conservative, the number was little more than academic with no boost specified, the same being true of the torque figure of 38 kg/m (275 lb/ft) at 9600 rpm. Informed sources

First pole position for turbo Renault was gained by Jabouille at Kyalami in 1979, although Ferrari 312 T4 won

Ferrari 312 T4 (Gilles Villeneuve shown winning Long Beach) was the outstanding car of 1979 Grand Prix season

Pages 37–37 Head-on shot at 1979 Zolder race contrasts RS 10 (15) with RS 01

Cutaway drawing of Renault RS 10, introduced in 1979. Note skirts, twin-turbo engine and biplane rear wing

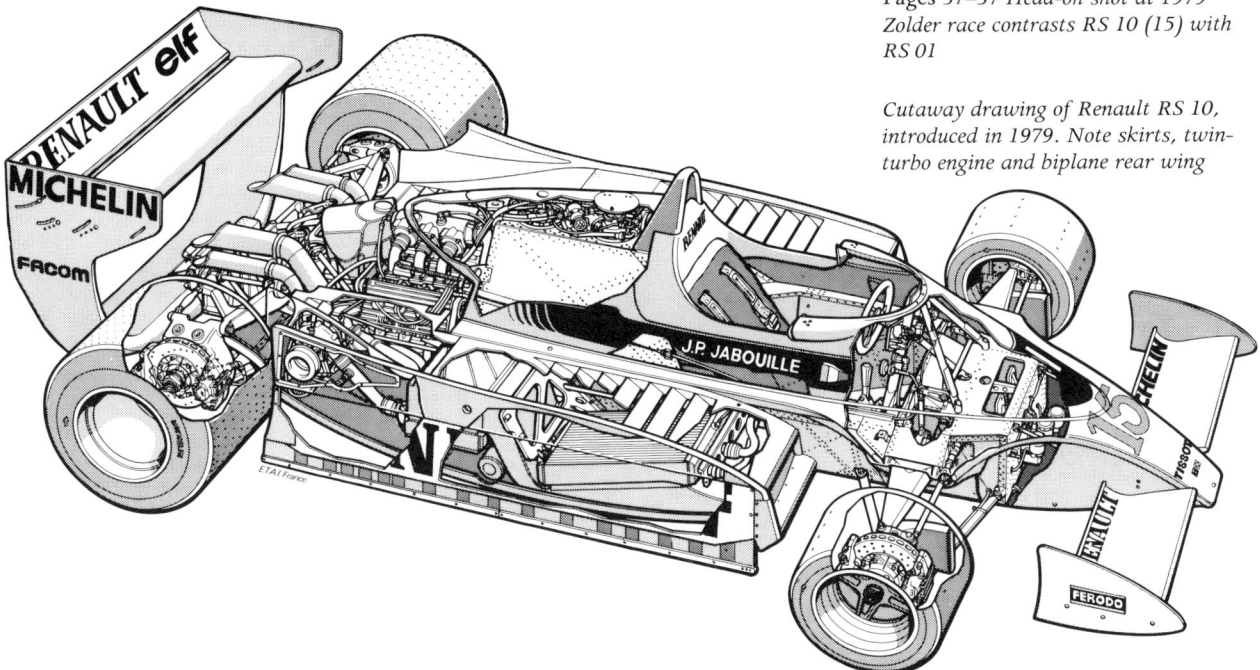

within the Formula 1 ranks (that is to say, the other drivers who watched the Renaults accelerate past on the straights!) put the figure at about 520 bhp, with close to 600 being realized with maximum boost. Jabouille and Arnoux continued as team-mates for 1980.

The cars retired in short order from the first Grand Prix in Argentina, but the team was in top form in Brazil and South Africa. At both circuits it was the team leader Jabouille who qualified on the pole, but it was Arnoux who won both events after Jabouille retired, also setting the fastest laps. And a Renault had been in the lead on every lap in both races. At that point Renault looked like a sure bet for the World Championship, with the little Arnoux finally coming into his own.

But then followed a series of six races in which the turbos were not fully competitive, on circuits which favored good handling more than horsepower. Jabouille's run of retirements continued; these included every major type of failure that was engine-related—clutch, gearbox, final drive, turbo and valve spring, the last-named occurring in a race which he at least had the satisfaction of leading, the German Grand Prix in early August. Arnoux could count two finishes in the points during this period, a fourth in Belgium and a fifth in France, but his initial championship lead was long gone.

Renault returned to form in Austria, the cars qualifying one-two and Jabouille enjoying a long-overdue victory. Arnoux, who had set the pole time and also had the fastest lap in the race, led the field for eighteen laps but eventually finished ninth, a lap down, after making three pit stops. The Renaults were quickest in practice for the next two races as well, Arnoux heading his team-mate at the front of the grid at Zandvoort and Imola. He led both events briefly, finishing second and scoring the fastest lap in the Dutch race, and ending up tenth, two laps behind, in the Italian Grand Prix. Jabouille's terrible luck continued, with retirements from final-drive and gearbox failures (or was he less sensitive to his equipment than Arnoux?). At Imola, in practice at least, Renault was joined by its first turbo rival, the Ferrari 126 C which Villeneuve qualified faster than his regular 312 T5 but did not race, leaving the direct confrontation for 1981.

The 1980 season ended badly for the French team, Jabouille being injured in a crash in the Canadian Grand Prix after qualifying only thirteenth fastest, and Arnoux qualifying a miserable twenty-third and dropping out at half distance. Jabouille was not entered at Watkins Glen and in fact did not drive for Renault again, although he recovered sufficiently to drive a few 1981 races for the Talbot-Ligier team. Finding himself uncompetitive, he wisely retired at midseason. But his career had included two important victories while at Renault, one of them the historic first turbo victory in Formula 1.

His place on the Renault team was taken by Alain Prost, an incredibly quick natural driver who had gained experience in a moderately successful 1980 season with McLaren and was now poised for better things. Unfortunately, half of the season would go by before Renault was again competitive, not to say reliable. The 20-series cars had been joined by RE 26B and 27B, number 22 also being brought up to 'B' configuration. Power was now officially quoted at 520 bhp at 10,500 rpm, again conservative.

As told in Chapter 4, Renault was temporarily overshadowed by

Opposite page, top René Arnoux joined Jabouille on the Renault team in 1979. Here he drives RS 10-01 at Monte Carlo

Opposite page, bottom Jabouille scored an historic first turbo victory in the French Grand Prix at Dijon in July 1979. The car was RS 10-02; Arnoux was third in RS 10-03 after a fierce battle with Villeneuve's Ferrari 312 T4

Renault staff at the factory in December 1979: from left, chassis designer Marcel Têtu, team manager Jean Sage, overall director Gerard Larrousse and technical director Bernard Dudot (also responsible for engine design)

A technician 'drives' a Renault turbo engine through simulated laps on the test bench in the Gordini plant at Viry-Châtillon, south of Paris

First of new RE 20 series was tested by Jabouille in November 1979

AV

41

AV

E.T.A.I France

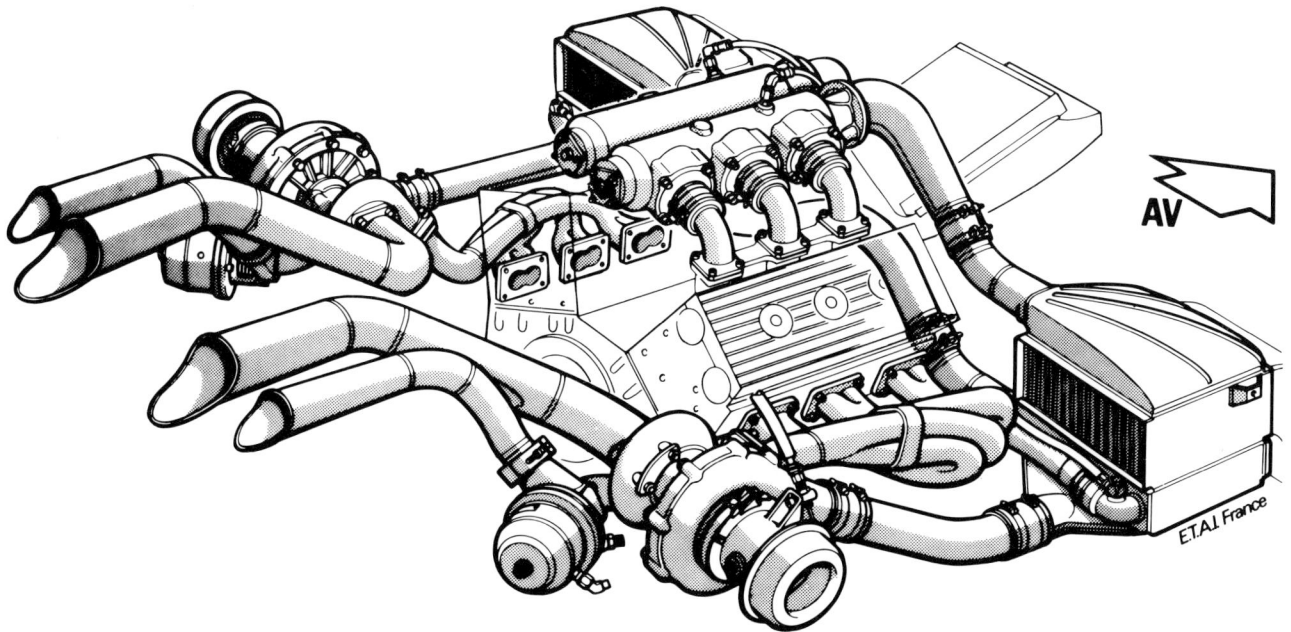

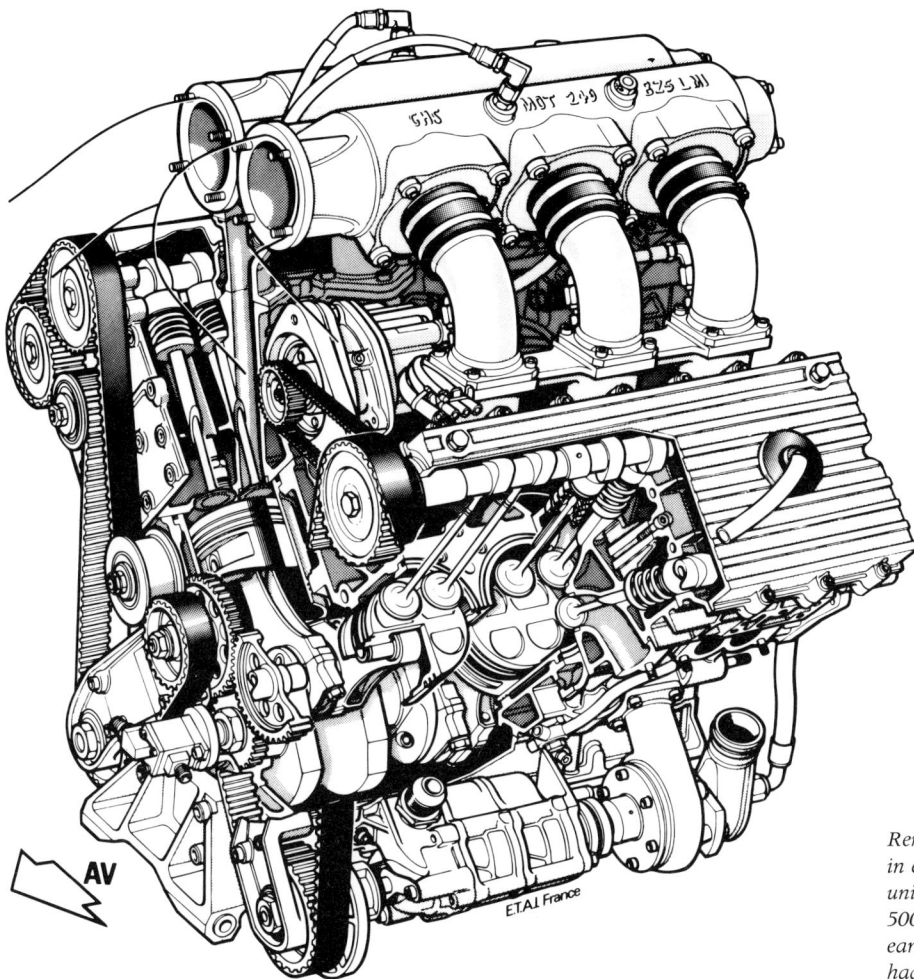

Renault 1.5-liter V-6 Formula 1 engine
in early-1980 configuration. Twin-turbo
unit produced a conservatively-estimated
500 bhp at 11,000 rpm at that time. By
early 1982 some 125 Gordini V-6 engines
had been built, 65 for Formula 1 use

*Arnoux winning the 1980 South African
Grand Prix in RE 21. He also won at
Rio and set fastest laps in both events*

Ferrari's quick turbo progress in the first half of the year. After six hard years developing its turbo Formula 1 cars to a state of competitiveness, Renault saw its Italian rival catch up, seemingly within months. But in fact, Ferrari's turbo program was three years old, the Scuderia waiting until the engine was more reliable before committing it to competition; this is no criticism of Renault, which needed an early entry into Formula 1 in order to learn the business of Grand Prix racing. The second half of 1981 vindicated Renault; their cars started from the pole in six consecutive Grands Prix and won three of them in the hands of the brilliant Prost, who established himself as *the* man to beat. Arnoux could match or exceed his qualifying times but did not approach his race consistency, five of Arnoux's seven retirements being from accidents. Renault's combination of engine power (about the same as Ferrari's) and chassis handling (far better than Ferrari's) made it the outstanding marque of 1981, even though the manufacturers' championship went to the very reliable Williams team and the driver's title to Nelson Piquet. The 30-series chassis (RE 30, 31, 32, 33, 34 and 35), introduced at Monte Carlo at the end of May, required several races before they were sorted but were the front-runners from the French Grand Prix onwards. With his three wins and 43 points, Prost placed fifth in the 1981 championship and started 1982 as the favorite.

He won the first two races of the year, Kyalami by being far and away the fastest man on the track, even though losing the lead to his team-mate temporarily when stopping to replace a punctured tire; Rio by having the highest-placed car not to be disqualified for arriving at the finish line below the minimum weight. After that, he was less fortunate, although still retaining his championship lead after six races. A Renault started from the pole in five of these six, Arnoux achieving this distinction on three occasions, but the team experienced nine retirements from its first twelve starts, six of these in accidents. Thirty kilograms lighter than the 1981 car at 595 kg, the RE 30B became the first Renault to approach the minimum weight figure of 580, even though the fuel capacity it required made starting-line weight greater than most of its rivals. With two new chassis built in 1982 and the six existing RE 30s brought up to 'B' configuration, the team adopted a new designation system: RE 30B-1 through 8.

At the time of writing, it appeared that Renault was still the most competitive car all around and that Prost was still the best bet for the champion. But despite this apparent form, the upheavals within Formula 1 have made everything uncertain. Given the continued participation of turbocharged engines in Grand Prix racing, it will be interesting to see which team gains the honor of winning the first turbo World Championship—Renault or Ferrari.

Car to beat in 1980 was Williams FW 07 of Alan Jones, contesting Zandvoort lead with Arnoux's Renault in photo opposite

45

Opposite, below Larrousse poses with his two drivers for 1981, the brilliant young Alain Prost (left), who replaced Jabouille, and René Arnoux, starting his third season

Arnoux tests the first of the RE 30 series at Paul Ricard. Note that both his name and that of Prost appear on the cowling, similar to Ferrari's custom for midwinter publicity photography

46

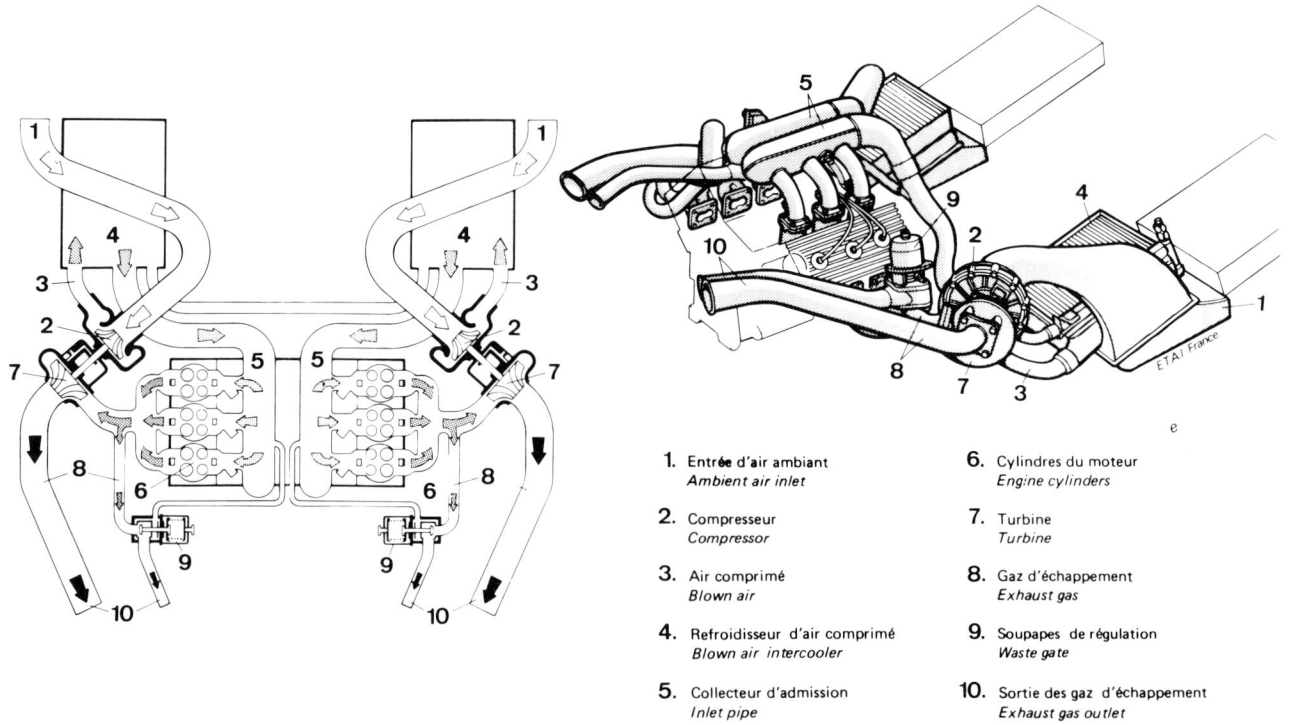

1. Entrée d'air ambiant
   Ambient air inlet

2. Compresseur
   Compressor

3. Air comprimé
   Blown air

4. Refroidisseur d'air comprimé
   Blown air intercooler

5. Collecteur d'admission
   Inlet pipe

6. Cylindres du moteur
   Engine cylinders

7. Turbine
   Turbine

8. Gaz d'échappement
   Exhaust gas

9. Soupapes de régulation
   Waste gate

10. Sortie des gaz d'échappement
    Exhaust gas outlet

Schematic drawing and perspective illustration

48

Right *the two Renaults head the 1981 Monza pack; Prost led all the way for his third win*

Below *cutaway drawing of RE 30 series chassis, and* right, *the same basic design in extensively revised RE 30B configuration for 1982. Note vertical side fairings, single-plane rear wing*

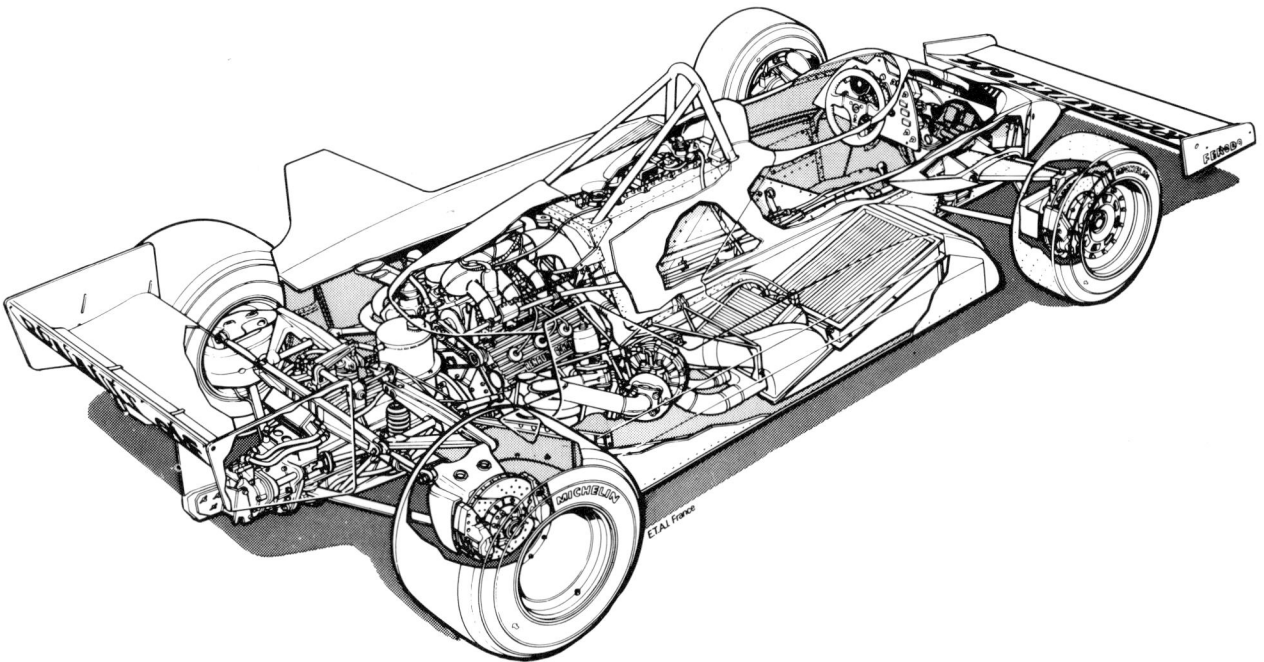

Renault Formula 1 Turbo Racing

Date	Race	Driver/Chassis/Qualifying position/Result
16/7/77	GB	Jabouille RS-01-1 Q21 R, turbo
28/8/77	NL	Jabouille RS-01-1 Q10 R, suspension
11/9/77	I	Jabouille RS-01-1 Q20 R, engine
2/10/77	USA/E	Jabouille RS-01-1 Q14 R, alternator
9/10/77	CDN	Jabouille RS-01-1 DNQ DNS
4/3/78	ZA	Jabouille RS-01-2 Q6 R, engine
2/4/78	USA/W	Jabouille RS-01-3 Q13 R, fire
7/5/78	MC	Jabouille RS-01-3 Q12 10th
21/5/78	B	Jabouille RS-01-2 Q10 Unclassified
4/6/78	E	Jabouille RS-01-3 Q11 13th
17/6/78	S	Jabouille RS-01-2 Q10 R, piston
2/7/78	F	Jabouille RS-01-2 Q11 R, engine
16/7/78	GB	Jabouille RS-01-3 Q12 R, engine
30/7/78	D	Jabouille RS-01-3 Q9 R, engine
13/8/78	A	Jabouille RS-01-2 Q3 R, gearbox
27/8/78	NL	Jabouille RS-01-2 Q9 R, piston
10/9/78	I	Jabouille RS-01-2 Q3 R, valve
1/10/78	USA/E	Jabouille RS-01-2 Q9 4th
8/10/78	CDN	Jabouille RS-01-2 Q22 12th
21/1/79	RA	Jabouille RS-01-4 Q12 R, engine; Arnoux RS-01-3 Q24 R, engine
4/2/79	BR	Jabouille RS-01-2 Q7 10th; Arnoux RS-01-3 Q11 R, spin
3/3/79	ZA	Jabouille RS-01-2 **Q1** R, valve spring; Arnoux RS-01-3 Q10 R, tire
8/4/79	USA/W	Jabouille RS-01-4 Q20 DNS; Arnoux RS-01-3 Q22 DNS
29/4/79	E	Jabouille RS 10 Q9 R, turbo; Arnoux RS-01-3 Q11 9th
13/5/79	B	Jabouille RS 10 Q17 R, turbo; Arnoux RS-01-3 Q18 R, turbo
27/5/79	MC	Jabouille RS 11 Q19 8th; Arnoux RS 10 Q20 R, steering
1/7/79	F	Jabouille RS 11 **Q1 1st**; Arnoux RS 12 Q2 3rd and **FL**
14/7/79	GB	Jabouille RS 11 Q2 R, valve spring; Arnoux RS 12 Q5 2nd
29/7/79	D	Jabouille RS 11 **Q1** R, accident; Arnoux RS 12 Q10 R, tire
12/8/79	A	Jabouille RS 11 Q3 R, clutch; Arnoux RS 12 **Q1** 6th and **FL**
26/8/79	NL	Jabouille RS 11 Q4 R, clutch; Arnoux RS 12 **Q1** R, accident
9/9/79	I	Jabouille RS 11 **Q1** 14th (n/r); Arnoux RS 12 Q2 R, electrics
30/9/79	CDN	Jabouille RS 14 Q7 R, brakes; Arnoux RS 12 Q8 R, accident
7/10/79	USA/E	Jabouille RS 14 Q8 R, camshaft belt; Arnoux RS 12 Q7 2nd
13/1/80	RA	Jabouille RE 22 Q9 R, clutch; Arnoux RE 21 Q19 R, suspension
27/1/80	BR	Jabouille RE 22 **Q1** R, turbo; Arnoux RE 21 Q6 **1st and FL**
1/3/80	ZA	Jabouille RE 23 **Q1** R, puncture; Arnoux RE 21 Q2 **1st and FL**

Performances, 1977 through June 1982

Date	Race	Driver/Chassis/Qualifying position/Result
30/3/80	USA/W	Jabouille RE 23 Q11 10th; Arnoux RE 24 Q2 9th
4/5/80	B	Jabouille RE 23 Q5 R, clutch; Arnoux RE 24 Q6 4th
18/5/80	MC	Jabouille RE 23 Q16 R, gearbox; Arnoux RE 24 Q20 R, accident
1/6/80	E	Jabouille RE 23 DNP DNS; Arnoux RE 24 DNP DNS
29/6/80	F	Jabouille RE 23 Q6 R, transmission; Arnoux RE 24 Q2 5th
13/7/80	GB	Jabouille RE 23 Q13 R, engine; Arnoux RE 22 Q16 Unclassified
10/8/80	D	Jabouille RE 23 Q2 R, valve spring; Arnoux RE 25 Q3 R, valve spring
17/8/80	A	Jabouille RE 23 Q2 **1st**; Arnoux RE 25 **Q1** 9th and **FL**
31/8/80	NL	Jabouille RE 23 Q2 R, differential; Arnoux RE 25 **Q1** 2nd and **FL**
14/9/80	I	Jabouille RE 23 Q2 R, gearbox; Arnoux RE 25 **Q1** 10th
28/9/80	CDN	Jabouille RE 23 Q13 R, accident; Arnoux RE 25 Q23 R, brakes
5/10/80	USA/E	Arnoux RE 25 Q6 7th
15/3/81	USA/W	Prost RE 26B Q14 R, accident; Arnoux RE 27B Q20 8th
29/3/81	BR	Prost RE 22B Q5 R, accident; Arnoux RE 26B Q8 R, accident
12/4/81	RA	Prost RE 22B Q2 3rd; Arnoux RE 27B Q5 5th
3/5/81	SM	Prost RE 22B Q4 R, gearbox; Arnoux RE 27B Q3 8th
17/5/81	B	Prost RE 22B Q12 R, clutch; Arnoux RE 27B DNQ DNS
31/5/81	MC	Prost RE 30 Q9 R, valve; Arnoux RE 27B Q13 R, accident
21/6/81	E	Prost RE 32 Q5 R, accident; Arnoux RE 33 Q17 9th
5/7/81	F	Prost RE 32 Q3 **1st and FL**; Arnoux RE 33 **Q1** 4th
18/7/81	GB	Prost RE 32 Q2 R, engine; Arnoux RE 33 **Q1** R, engine; **FL**
2/8/81	D	Prost RE 32 **Q1** 2nd; Arnoux RE 33 Q2 13th
16/8/81	A	Prost RE 32 Q2 R, suspension; Arnoux RE 31 **Q1** 2nd
30/8/81	NL	Prost RE 34 **Q1** **1st**; Arnoux RE 33 Q2 R, accident
13/9/81	I	Prost RE 34 Q3 **1st**; Arnoux RE 33 **Q1** R, accident
27/9/81	CDN	Prost RE 34 Q4 R, accident; Arnoux RE 33 Q8 R, accident
17/10/81	USA/LV	Prost RE 34 Q5 2nd; Arnoux RE 35 Q13 R, engine
23/1/82	ZA	Prost RE 30B-5 Q5 **1st and FL**; Arnoux RE 30B-6 **Q1** 3rd
21/3/82	BR	Prost RE 30B-6 **Q1** **1st***; Arnoux RE 30B-7 Q4 R, accident
4/4/82	USA/W	Prost RE 30B-6 Q4 R, accident; Arnoux RE 30B-7 Q3 R, accident
25/4/82	SM	Prost RE 30B-8 Q2 R, engine; Arnoux RE 30B-7 **Q1** R, engine
9/5/82	B	Prost RE 30B-8 **Q1** R, accident; Arnoux RE 30B-7 Q2 R, turbo
23/5/82	MC	Prost RE 30B-8 Q4 R, accident; Arnoux RE 30B-7 **Q1** R, spin
6/6/82	USA/D	Prost RE 30B-6 **Q1** 12th; Arnoux RE 30B-7 Q15 10th
13/6/82	CDN	Prost RE 30B-6 Q3 R, engine; Arnoux RE 30B-7 Q2 R, spin

Key: RS, Renault Sport; RE, Renault Elf; Q, qualifying position; R, retired; DNP, did not practice; DNQ did not qualify; DNS, did not start; (n/r), not running at finish; FL, fastest lap; *Finished 3rd but classified 1st after first two disqualified

51

Chapter 3
the 126 C

RENAULT'S EXPERIENCE had shown that the development of a competitive turbocharged Formula 1 car was expensive, long and difficult. Ferrari's experience in Grand Prix racing—over thirty years of continuous competition—could be counted upon to avoid some of the problems encountered by the French team, while the Maranello engine design staff was acknowledged to be second to none. The Ferrari engineers also had the advantage of anticipating the mechanical failures that had already plagued the Renault program; the actual technical solutions would be different, of course, but much of the turbo groundwork had been done. Working directly with KKK, Ferrari had the opportunity to design a completely new engine for Grand Prix racing, their first since the Boxer flat-12, conceived ten years earlier.

There were two major reasons for Ferrari's decision to take the turbo path. The most obvious was that, ultimately, far greater power could be produced by the boosted 1.5-liter then the normally-aspirated 3-liter— perhaps in excess of 700 bhp after several years of constant development. The second, more immediate, reason was the practical need for a narrower engine to take advantage of the ground-effect technology that was just coming into use in Formula 1 in 1978, a rush to slim monocoques with wing-profiled sidepods in imitation of Colin Chapman's revolutionary Lotus. This technology, with its sliding or non-sliding skirts, would cause more controversy and rule-bending than any previous Formula 1 confrontation, but no team could afford to ignore its benefit of phenomenally high corning speeds.

The Ferrari design team, headed by Ing. Mauro Forghieri and including Franco Rocchi, Walter Salvarani and Angiolino Marchetti, was backed up by the technical resources and testing laboratories of the entire Fiat organization as well as by all the related component manufacturers and suppliers. Preliminary studies began in 1977 and it didn't take long for the V-6 configuration to be selected: initial detail design started the following year. While the previous Dino V-6 designs could not really be used as models for the new engine with its completely different requirements (not to mention a power output from two to three times greater), the advantages of a short, strong crankshaft and a direct, compact turbo routing were certainly the deciding factors.

Power meant heat, and turbo pressures compounded the problems of component reliability. Ferrari had always built robust engines with admirable records for reliability, but Maranello was taking on a new set of problems with the turbo. In addition to the boost range from high

Debut of 126 C at Fiorano in June 1980; car carried Scheckter's number 1 on the left side and Villeneuve's number 2 on the right (see page 54). First car, 047, had characteristic spine-like fairing over engine cover. Quoted power was 540 bhp

Engineer Mauro Forghieri holds forth for journalists at press showing of 126 C. Car bore some external resemblance to 312 T5 but was much more aerodynamic

Last boxer 312, the T5 of 1980, suffered from Ferrari's concentration on new turbo design

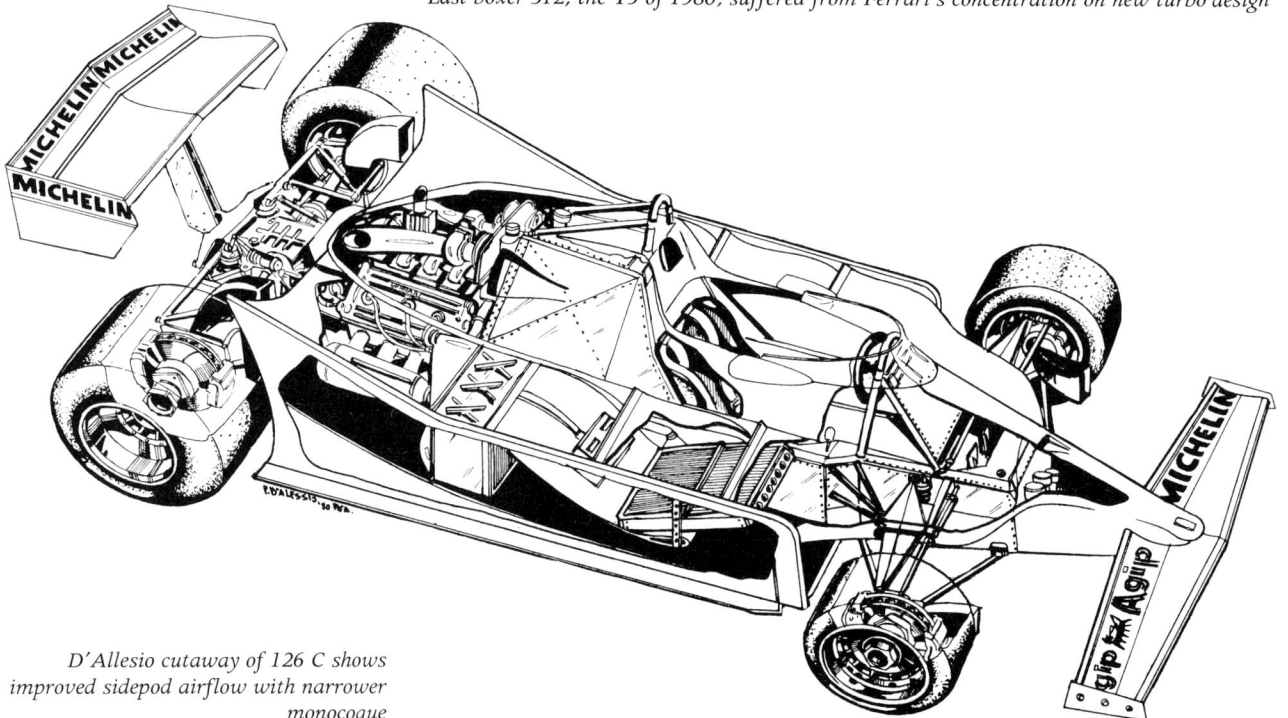

D'Allesio cutaway of 126 C shows improved sidepod airflow with narrower monocoque

(for maximum power output, especially in qualification) to moderate (for race-distance reliability), the abnormally high fuel consumption of the turbo system and its elevated cylinder-head temperatures had to be dealt with. Most racing turbos have used intercoolers between the exhaust-driven turbines and the induction manifolding. On the Ferrari arrangement the six exhaust pipes within the vee fed through a wastegate to twin turbos mounted on top of the engine at the front; from here the charged air passed through the intercoolers, mounted one at each side of the chassis monocoque ahead of the engine, and then back to the intake manifold 'logs' at the outside of each bank of cylinders. Being only a 1.5-liter six, the actual engine was extremely compact, but the required turbo plumbing was a challenge for effective chassis layout.

The dimensions finally selected for the V-6, after single-cylinder tests of several combinations, were a bore of 81 mm and a stroke of 48.4 mm (compared to 80×49.6 for the contemporary 312 Boxer Formula 1 engine with twice as many cylinders). This gave a capacity of 1496.43 cm^3. As with the Formula 1 Dino engine of 1961–1964, the angle of the vee was 120 degrees, but there was little similarity beyond that. Four valves and a single spark plug per cylinder were used, as with the 312 Boxers, while the compression ratio was only 6.5:1 (compared to 11.5:1 on the 312 T4 and T5) because of the turbo.

Engines went on to the dynamometers at Maranello in 1979, as chassis design proceeded. This was the year that the 312 T4 was winning Ferrari's most recent World Championship and it was impressive that the factory could devote so much engineering time to the new project while being so effectively committed to the job at hand. In fact, the cost (to the development of the current machinery) became apparent the following year, when the reigning championship team had an absolutely miserable season with the 312 T5. By 1980 the ground-effect systems, with sliding skirts, had become so highly developed by Ferrari's rivals that the T5 with its wide Boxer engine could not match their adhesion. The reigning champion, Jody Scheckter, was not particularly disturbed as he was already contemplating his retirement from competition. On the other hand, Gilles Villeneuve, never content at even a fraction of a second below his potential, had the power of the new turbo to look forward to.

In June 1980 Ferrari unveiled its all-new car to the press at the factory's Fiorano test track, located to the northwest of the Maranello plant on the opposite side of the road to Modena, the firm's traditional home. It was the first 1.5-liter car and the first Formula 1 V-6 from Ferrari since 1965 (not counting the 2.4 Tasman version of the Dino engine used in several races in 1966). It was called the 126 C, for 120-degree six, with *compressore* (supercharger). The selection of this designation, rather than the expected 156 (1.5-liter six), showed a possible unwillingness to link the car with the earlier Dino, or perhaps a sentimental wish on the part of Enzo Ferrari to relate it to the original Formula 1 Ferrari, the supercharged 125 F1 of 1958–1950. Ferrari has always enjoyed playing with numbers, in designations as well as in technology.

The 126 C carried number 1 and Jody Scheckter's name (he was destined to test it several times, but never to race it) on its left side and

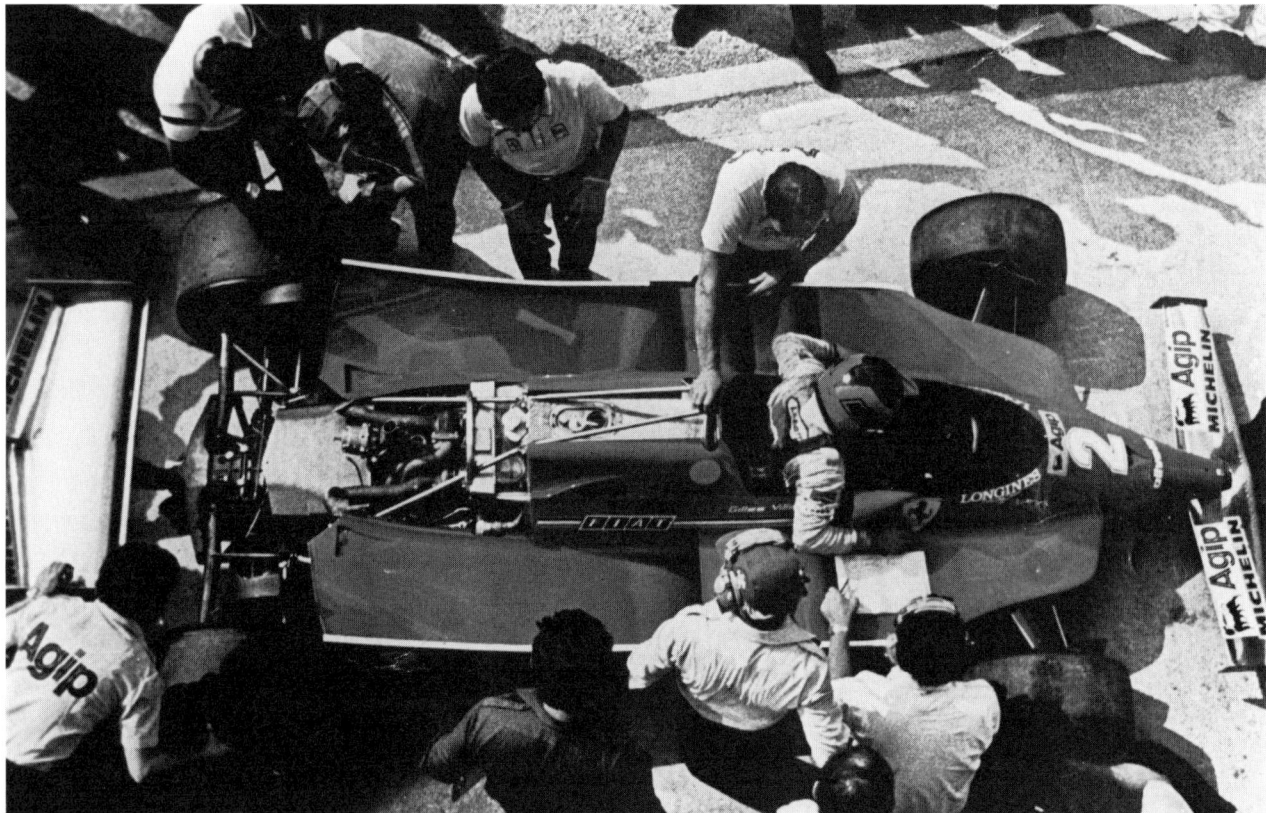

number 2 and Gilles Villeneuve's name on the right. As revealed to the press, this first turbo (chassis 047, falling between the next-to-last and last of the 312 T5s, rather than starting a new series as would have been expected) was a tidy machine, vastly cleaned up in comparison with the T5 but showing some visual similarity. For the first time since 1973, the front wing grew out of the sides of the nose cone rather than being mounted full-width above it. The sidepods, employing sliding skirts (still legal in 1980), resembled those of the earlier machine externally but were wider and had much improved airflow inside.

The headrest fairing extended well to the rear, giving a finned appearance. Under this fairing (separately removable rather than part of the cockpit cover) sat Forghieri's new creation, the tiny but already potent-looking turbocharged engine. With the initial KKK turbos, the plumbing above the wide-angle 24-valve V-6 dominated the engine compartment. A figure of 540 bhp at 11,000 rpm was given, with a 6.5:1 compression ratio, in the small brochure handed out to the press. Compared to the figure of 515 bhp at 12,300 rpm at 11.5:1 for the 312 T4 and T5, this was a healthy increase (in retrospect, perhaps even a little on the conservative side). But the problem of throttle lag plus the high stress and heat factors could be expected to limit the turbo's effectiveness at first, as had been Renault's experience.

A redesigned version of Ferrari's very successful transverse gearbox and final drive was employed, with five or six speeds. The suspension consisted of inboard coil springs operated by rocker arms, front and rear, and the brakes were outboard on all four wheels. The water radiator was located obliquely in the left-hand sidepod, near the front, with the oil radiator in the corresponding position on the right; as mentioned, the intercoolers were mounted amidships behind them. A very round figure of 600 kg, equivalent to 1323 pounds, was quoted for the car's total weight, exclusive of fuel and driver. Ferrari has been a bit more realistic in this department recently, especially compared to wildly optimistic figures given for cars in the past, but the number had to be taken as an approximation, at least until the car was fully sorted.

Testing continued at Fiorano and changes became apparent almost immediately. At the car's public debut, in practice for the Italian Grand Prix at Imola in September, it showed revised suspension geometry, a different wastegate position (vertical rather than horizontal), vertical rather than oblique intercoolers, and an engine cover that sloped down in back, looking more like those of the Boxers and losing some of the prototype's distinctive appearance. At Imola this 126 C (chassis 049, the second) carried number 2 and was driven in spirited fashion by Villeneuve during practice, even though it was not intended that the turbo be raced. The performance was partly to keep faith with the Italian fans, who were not at all pleased by the T5's dismal record, and partly an opportunity for Gilles to relieve his frustrations. The Canadian had been very diplomatic about not criticizing the T5 throughout the season. Fortified by 750 miles of testing the new car at Fiorano, his hopes for the turbo helped to sustain his morale. As a teaser for 1981, he lapped Imola in 1:35.751, six-tenths of a second faster than he was able to achieve in his regular T5, and he gained the eighth-fastest starting position with this time, although using the T5 for the race. It was a promising debut.

Second 126 C, chassis 049, was driven in practice for 1980 Italian Grand Prix by Villeneuve, but it was mainly a demonstration for the crowd and the turbo debut did not come until 1981 at Long Beach

59

Villeneuve (getting into car in center *photo below) did most of 126 C testing at Fiorano in winter of 1980–1981 but Scheckter (*opposite page, top and center*) drove the turbo a few times before his retirement. His 1981 replacement, Didier Pironi, is shown at* bottom left. *Comprex-supercharged version was also tested extensively; Villeneuve is shown with this unit in photo at* bottom *of this page*

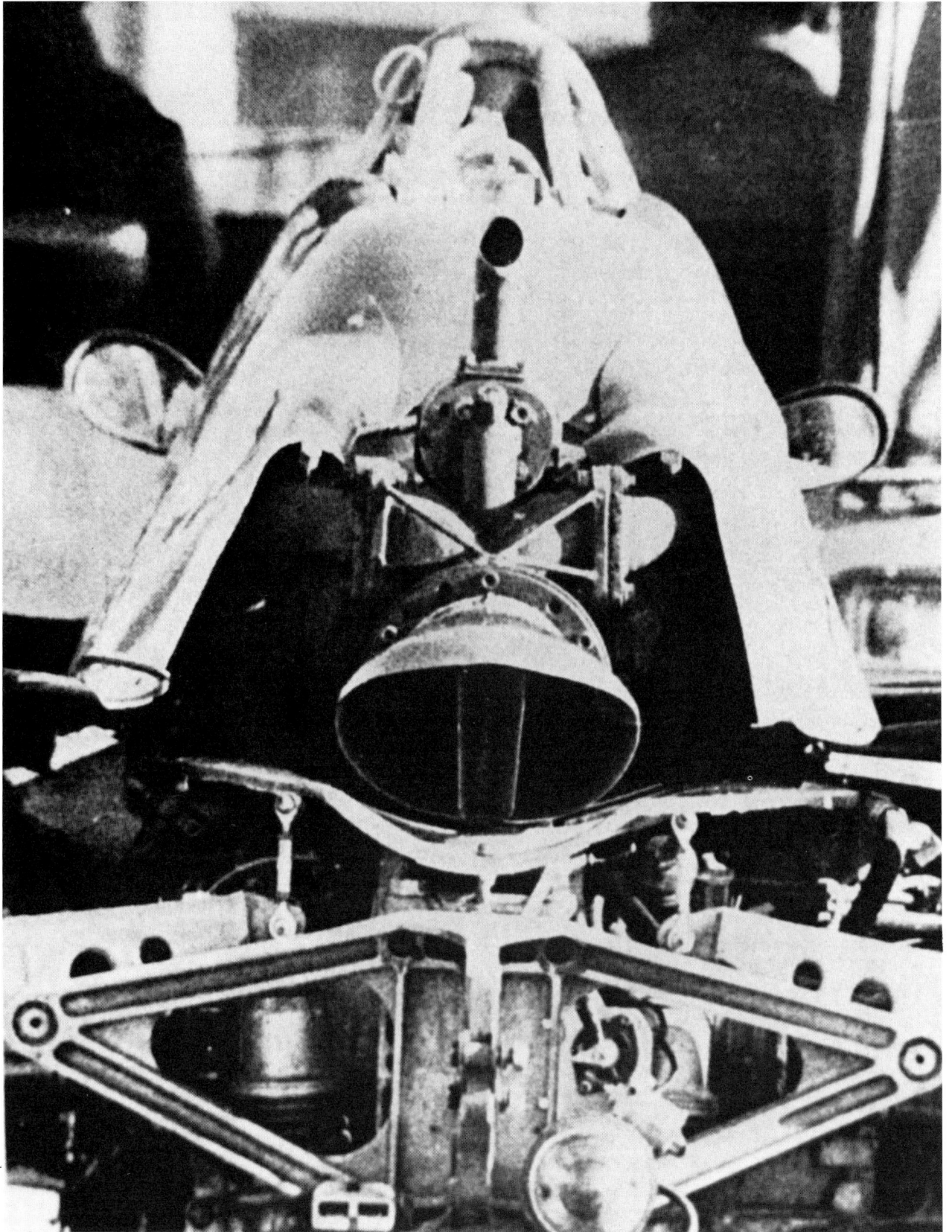

The fall of 1980 through the spring of 1981 saw intense political battles waged between FISA (*Fédération Internationale Sport Automobile*) and FOCA (Formula One Constructors Association) for the control of Grand Prix racing, the first of a seemingly endless series of squabbles that has given the concept of sportsmanship a near death blow and offended almost everyone interested in Formula 1, especially the commercial sponsors and the paying public. All the teams continued testing, and development of the 126 C went on at an unrelenting pace. Villeneuve was joined at Ferrari by the French driver Didier Pironi, replacing the departing Scheckter. Pironi did some testing in the 312 T5 at Fiorano, probably not with any intention of it being raced in 1981; more likely it was a vehicle for him to familiarize himself with Fiorano before progressing to the 126 C and its different driving characteristics. Villeneuve did most of the turbo testing until the first of the year, by which time the KKK turbo system was joined by an entirely new development, the Comprex supercharger.

Exhaust pipe of Comprex-supercharged 126 engine, opposite, was a single megaphone

Specifications—1980 126 C

Engine: *120-degree V-6, mounted ahead of and driving rear wheels. Bore 81 mm, stroke 48.4 mm, displacement 1496.43 cm³. Gear-driven twin overhead camshafts for each bank of cylinders, operating two intake and two exhaust valves per cylinder. KKK turbocharger. Lucas fuel injection. Ignition by Marelli transistor. Single spark plug per cylinder. Compression ratio 6.5:1. Power output 540 bhp at 11,000 rpm. Specific output 360.6 bhp/liter.*
Transmission: *Dry multi-plate clutch between engine and gearbox. 5 and 6-speed and reverse gearbox mounted transversely behind engine in unit with final drive.*
Chassis: *Aluminum monocoque. Fiberglass body panels. Side fairings giving aerodynamic downforce, with sliding skirts. Fuel tank capacity 215 liters (56.8 U.S. gallons).*
Suspension: *Front, upper rocker arms, inboard coil spring/shock absorber units, wide base lower A-arms, anti-roll bar. Rear, halfshafts with constant-velocity joints, upper rocker arms, inboard coil spring/shock absorber units, lower links, anti-roll bar. Lockheed ventilated disc brakes, mounted outboard front and rear. Center-lock Speedline cast magnesium-alloy 13-inch wheels with Michelin radial tires.*
Dimensions: *Wheelbase 2719 mm (107.0 inches). Track 1761 mm (69.3 inches) front, 1626 (64.0 inches) rear. Length 4468 mm (175.9 inches). Width 2110 mm (83.1 inches). Height, to rollbar, 1025 mm (40.3 inches). Weight, less fuel and driver, 600 kg (1323 pounds). Weight/power ratio 1.11 kg (2.44 pounds)/bhp.*
Note: *Specifications based on Ferrari press release for original car. All figures potentially variable, especially those for track and width, dependent of wheels and tires mounted, and weight. Chassis numbers 047 and 049*

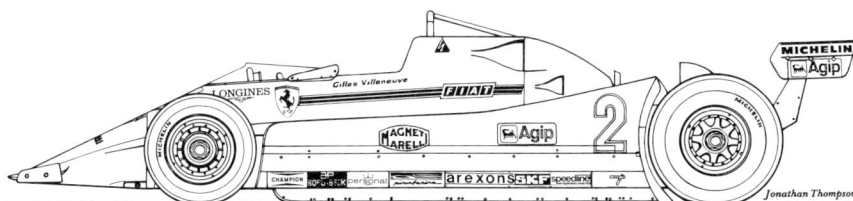

1980 126 C as driven by Gilles Villeneuve in practice at Imola (1/40 scale)

Color
Ferrari turbo salon

*First appearance of Ferrari turbo engine
was at Imola in September 1980. At that
time the 126 C produced 540 bhp*

*Villeneuve drove the 126 C in practice at
Imola, lapping faster than in his 312 T5,
but used the older car for the race*

Villeneuve lifts a front wheel at Long Beach in 1981. He tried Comprex supercharged and KKK turbo engines in practice

Overhead shot of Gilles' 126 C at Long Beach shows ducting in the tops of sidepods used early in the 1981 season

66

Villeneuve's enthusiasm, turbo power and 126 C's poor handling got him off track often, as here with Rebaque

Opposite page, top Villeneuve's win at Monte Carlo was welcome if not convincing. Bottom Revised monocoque and new front wing were used from mid-1981

Carma 308 GTB Biturbo, seen in pits at Mugello, was driven by Facetti/Finotto in most 1981 Group 5 events

With over 750 bhp available, Carma Biturbo was incredibly fast but seldom lasted more than a few laps

68

Factory tested KKK-boosted 2-liter GTB and GTS (shown) at Fiorano in 1981–1982 in development of first production turbo

Opposite page Special BAE turbocharged BB 512 had masterful detailing to match its 600-bhp output on 10-psi boost

Opposite page *Tomaini checks test record as Villeneuve prepares to leave pits for practice at Osterreichring in 1981*

Comprex-supercharged version, the 126 CX, was tested extensively, tried in practice at Long Beach in 1981, but never raced

Shown being unloaded from Ferrari transporter at Hockenheim in 1981, 1.5-liter V-6 engine is a very compact unit

KKK two-stage turbo 126 C3 engine produced 580–600 bhp at 11,000 rpm by early 1982 (Long Beach shown)

Top *BBC press photo of 126 CX was released early in 1981; note rough bodywork*

Bottom *Comprex-supercharged engines were tried in practice for Long Beach race*

Chapter 4
the Comprex supercharged 126 CX and KKK turbocharged 126 CK

TESTED ALMOST DAILY at Fiorano in the winter of 1980–1981, the 126 C was subjected to a continual program of small but important revisions. These were made to the suspension, aerodynamics and brakes, the last being a serious problem on the extremely fast but still overweight car. Pironi joined Villeneuve in the development driving and his times were soon in the same bracket, marginally slower than the Canadian's in most cases and occasionally faster, depending on the modifications being tested. The lap record at Fiorano, previously held by the 312 T5, was lowered repeatedly by the 126 C.

Significantly, more attention was given to engine development than to that of the chassis. This was understandable, considering Ferrari's emphasis on engine reliability and the need to make the complicated turbo system work at near-maximum boost for as many miles as possible, always considering the trade-off between power and fuel efficiency. If the engine were capable of lasting 200 miles at a certain boost, there was still the extra weight of fuel required for that output, possibly negating the power advantage. This differed according to the number of gear changes per lap and the seconds spent at maximum revolutions at a given circuit; in this respect the Fiorano track was invaluable, having been designed to simulate portions of the various tracks on which Ferrari raced during the season. In addition, there was the problem of testing without the skirts which increased the downforce generated by the sidepod aerodynamics; the whole question of skirts was one of the major items of contention in the FISA-FOCA dispute and none of the chassis designers could be sure of the form in which the cars would ultimately be allowed to run. Nevertheless, on 11 January Villeneuve drove a lap at Fiorano in 1:10.19, this being the best so far by a car without skirts (the Fiorano record with skirts was established by Scheckter in a T5 in 1980 at 1:08.74).

During this session Villeneuve tested an entirely new boost system developed by Brown, Boveri & Co. of Baden, Switzerland. Called the Comprex, it was a pressure-exchange system which promised equal power to that of the KKK turbo with significantly reduced throttle-lag. Villeneuve put in forty laps with the Comprex-equipped 126 C, encountering no serious problems and eventually recording a time of 1:10.61. The Comprex system used exhaust energy as did the turbocharger and was engine-driven like the supercharger, but was not strictly one nor the other. Basically, it was an exchanger of pressure

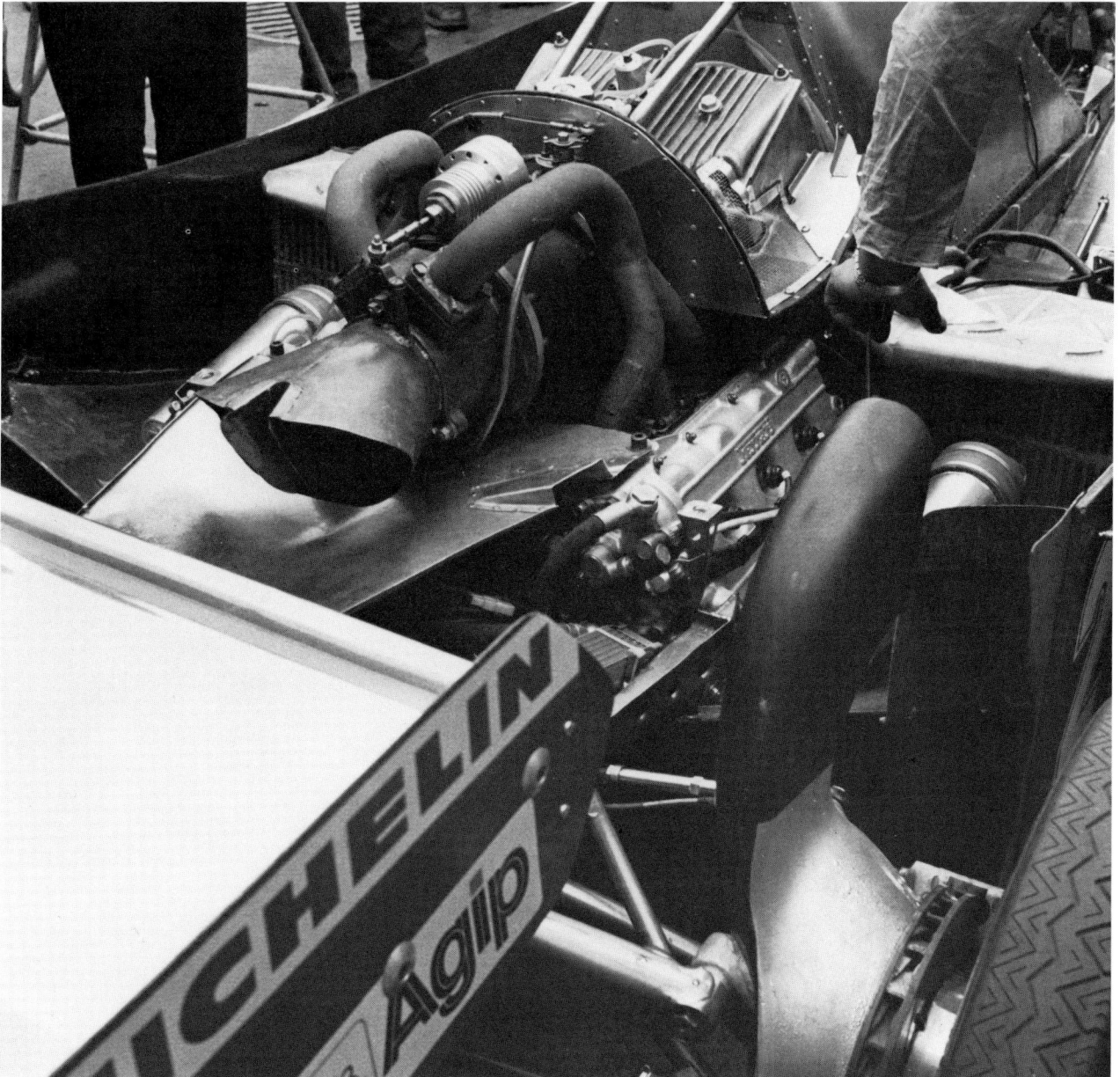

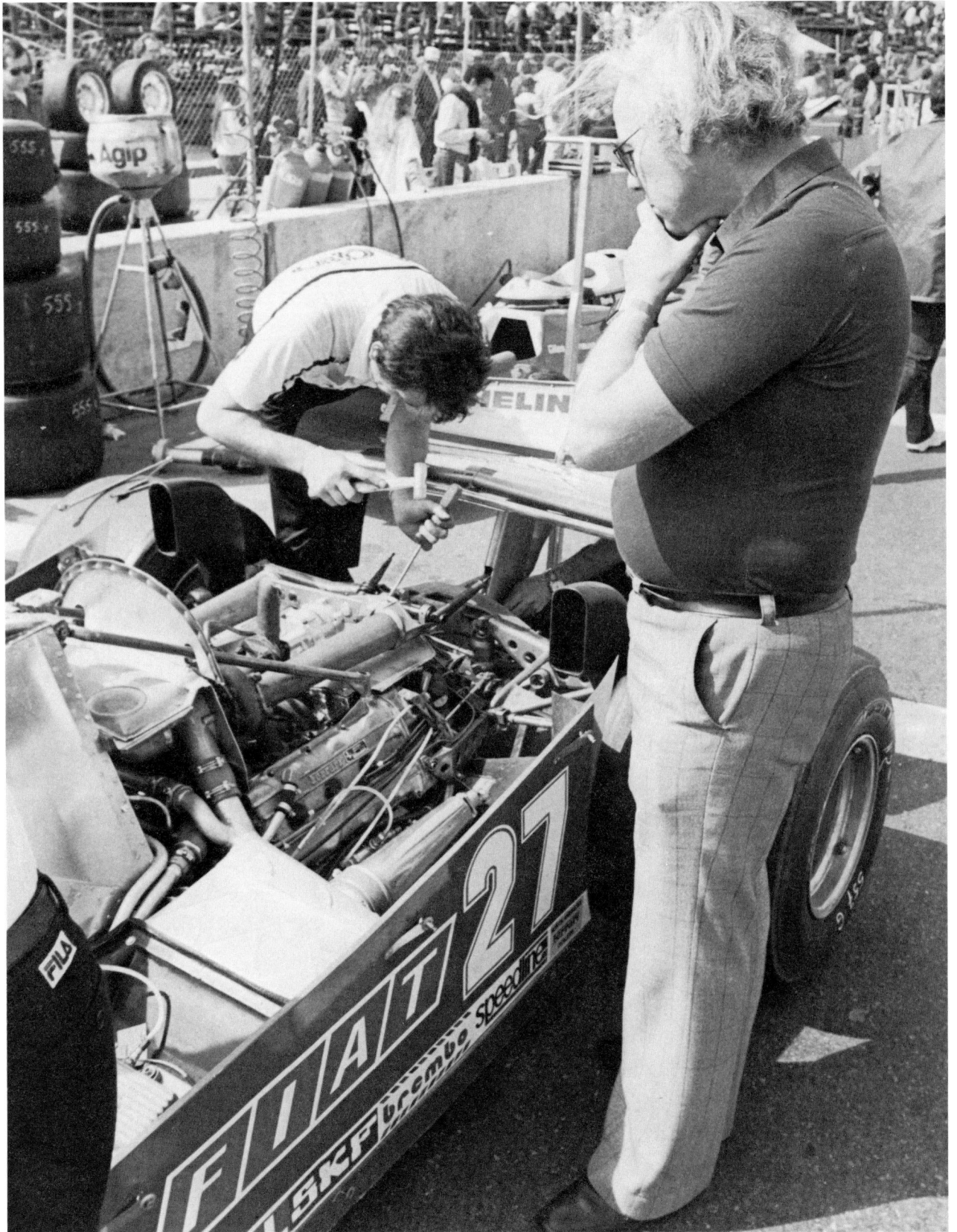

waves. A cylindrical rotor consisting of cells arranged axially revolved in a housing that had two end plates, one drawing engine intake air into and out of the housing, the other connected to the exhaust flow. As the engine-driven rotor revolved it mixed the high-pressure exhaust gas with the intake air, forcing the air into the combustion chamber at an increased density. The exhaust gas and intake air moved back and forth in each cell as the pressure energy was transferred. Brown, Boveri & Co. had been testing this system for about fifteen years on large engines, entering into a cooperative program with Ferrari in 1979.

Both of Ferrari's drivers were pleased with the lack of discernable delay in throttle response with the Comprex engines. Further tests were conducted at the Paul Ricard circuit in France, where Villeneuve was the fastest of all the cars present, even though times were generally slow because of the cold weather. Tony Kollbrunner, head of BBC's Comprex Development Turbomachinery Laboratory, felt that the system would be ideal for the Long Beach race in March; on that circuit instant acceleration was more important than peak power. As it turned out, the South African Grand Prix lost its championship status because of the ongoing FISA-FOCA dispute, and the California race saw the actual competition debut of the 126 C.

With the Comprex installed, a smaller wastegate and a simpler exhaust system was seen, characterized by a large, oval-section megaphone-shaped pipe pointing straight out the back. Other changes (with either engine) included new ducting into the sidepods, with the front suspension fairing no longer continuing into the upper surface of the body, which employed three airfoil-shaped vanes at the front of each sidepod. (Tests had already been conducted using sidepods with smooth upper surfaces and the air exhausting further back, and these would be adopted later in the season.)

The engine cover changed shape according to whether the Comprex or the KKK-equipped engine was installed, and the continued development of the turbocharger was not abated. Villeneuve and Pironi tested the cars exhaustively at Fiorano and Paul Ricard, the French driver usually in the KKK car. Compared to a time of 1:08.96 driven by Pironi in a skirted T5 for evaluation, Villeneuve established a Fiorano circuit record of 1:08.469 in a skirted 126. The best time there for a skirtless 126 had been 1:10.44, later reduced to the 1:10.2 bracket in a Comprex-equipped car by both drivers. At Ricard the best 126 time was Pironi's 1:05.67, compared to the fastest time of 1:04.77 set by Bruno Giacomelli's Alfa Romeo 179C V-12, so Ferrari still had a way to go before becoming fully competitive. During the development period *Autosprint* magazine had referred to the KKK-equipped car as the 126 K and the Comprex as the 126 C, while a factory release referred to the latter as the 126 BBC (Brown Boveri Comprex). Ultimately, the designations became 126 CK and 126 CX respectively, certainly more logical as the letter C denoted *compressore* in either case.

As the date of the first official World Championship points race at Long Beach approached, the cars neared their definitive configuration, with longer engine covers almost restoring the appearance of the press-debut car nine months before, and new, large 'Ferrari' and 'FIAT' lettering decorating the flanks. Carrying numbers 27 and 28 (inherited from Williams when that team took over 1 and 2 as a result of Alan

Opposite 'Hmmm, may have to make one of those if they don't change the equivalency.' Keith Duckworth looks at KKK-turbocharged Ferrari 126 CK engine at Long Beach

77

Pages 78–79 Villeneuve practices in Comprex-supercharged 126 CX at Long Beach

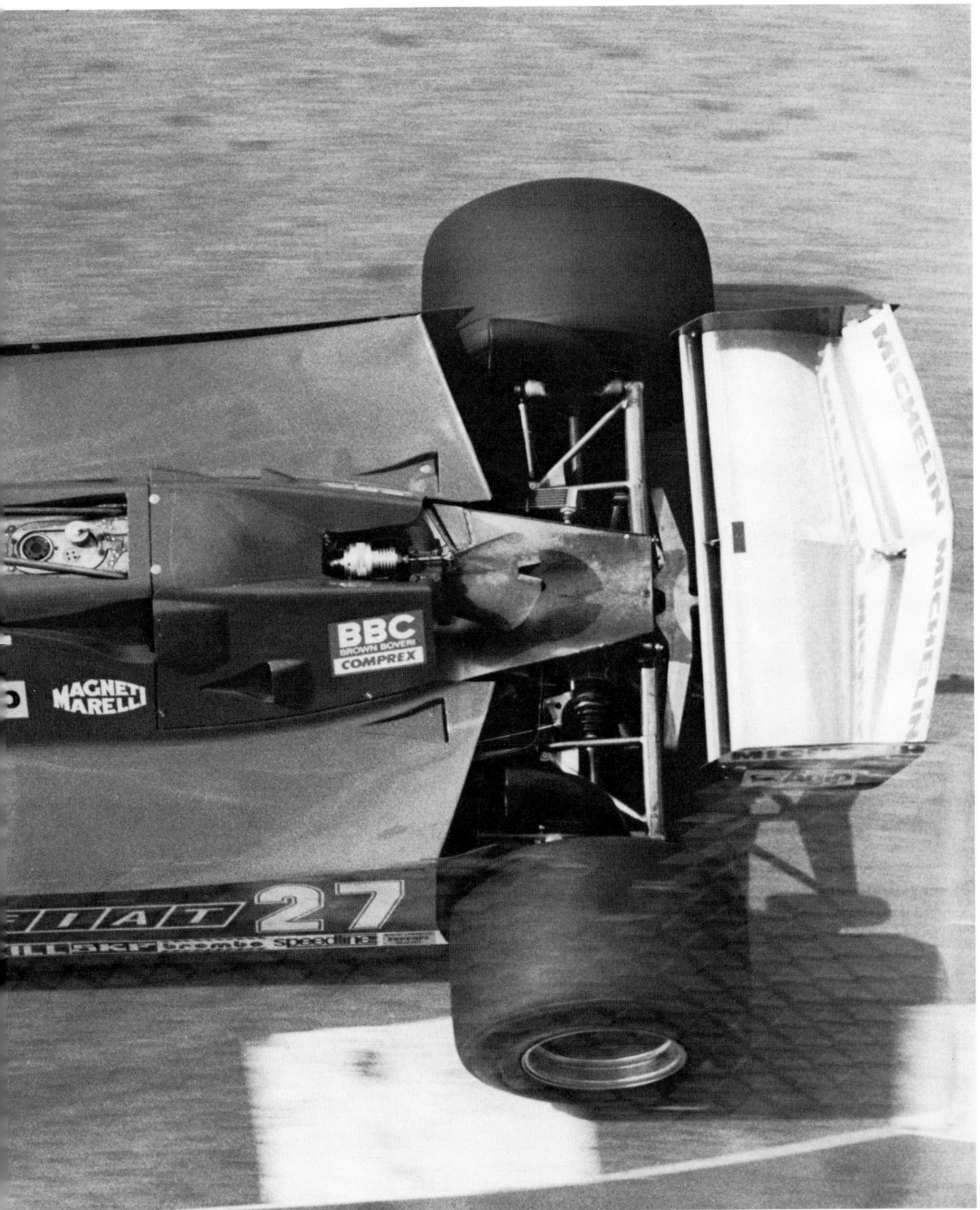

Denis Jenkinson takes notes as team manager Tomaini makes point on preparation

With KKK turbochargers, 126 engines had two short exhaust pipes coming out top

At rear, 126 had inboard springs and shock absorbers operated by rocker arms

Jones' 1980 title), the cars were shipped to the United States. Three chassis were prepared: 049 and 051 with Comprex engines and 050 with the KKK.

As practiced initially at Long Beach, Villeneuve's number 27 was a Comprex, while two cars, one of each type, carried Pironi's number 28. The Ferraris were slow to reach competitive times. In the Friday morning unofficial session Pironi and Villeneuve were eight and tenth fastest with times of 1:22.966 and 1:23.224 respectively. At the end of the afternoon qualifying period, after trying both the Comprex and the KKK systems, they had made substantial improvements, Villeneuve moving up to third best with 1:21.723 and Pironi, almost as fast, fifth with 1:21.828. It was the reigning champion Jones who set the pace in his Williams FW 07 Cosworth V-8.

The Ferrari drivers went around the 2.02-mile course a little quicker on Saturday, Villeneuve in 1:20.462 and Pironi in 1:20.909, but improvements by their competitors (Riccardo Patrese surprising everyone by qualifying his Arrows-Cosworth on the pole) meant that the Ferraris started fifth and eleventh. In comparison to the howl of the old flat-12 engines, the Comprex-equipped V-6 Ferraris had a much subdued, whistling sound, while the KKK cars were characterized by a deep, firecracker-like backfire on the overrun; the Alfa Romeo and Matra V-12s now provided the most audible exhaust notes, the latter being the most piercing.

After all the publicity concerning the Comprex system and its reduced throttle lag, it was the KKK system which produced the most power and the quickest lap times in practice, and both cars starting the race (049 and 051) used turbos. On the first lap Villeneuve and Pironi made good use of their acceleration on Shoreline Drive, coming around in fourth and sixth positions, sandwiching Nelson Piquet's Brabham-Cosworth, on the first lap. The order of this trio was reversed when Villeneuve braked late for the Queen's Hairpin and overshot, Pironi passing both him and Piquet. Patrese and the two Williams cars of Carlos Reutemann and Jones were already moving away up front; in the next group the order was Pironi, Piquet, Villeneuve, Eddie Cheever in a Tyrrell-Cosworth and Mario Andretti in an Alfa Romeo.

Villeneuve's 126 C was missing on lap 18, having suffered a broken driveshaft, but Pironi kept the other Ferrari ahead of Piquet for many laps until fuel vaporization began to affect his engine. First Piquet, next Cheever and then Andretti passed Pironi, the Alfa Romeo staying ahead only after a long battle during which the straightaway speed of the 126 C was sufficient to make up for the time lost on the tighter parts of the circuit. This duel between two Italian cars was probably the most exciting aspect of the Long Beach race.

Jones eventually won the race after Patrese retired and Reutemann slowed. Pironi's fuel problem finally caused his retirement after 66 laps, at which point he was in tenth position but not classified as a finisher, not having covered 90 percent of race distance. But he had driven an excellent debut race for Ferrari.

Both 126 C cars had shown real speed and the retirements were not unexpected for a new design. On the other hand, the cars were definitely overweight at 610 kg (1345 pounds), compounding the problems of braking and acceleration, and the handling was clearly not

Villeneuve made his usual charge from drop of flag at Long Beach but arrived at first turn too fast and had to go wide. Patrese, in Ragno Arrows, took an early lead

Pironi's first race for Ferrari at Long Beach was a promising one, but fuel vaporization eventually made him stop

Ferraris were not competitive at Rio de Janeiro; Villeneuve bent front and rear wings at start, fought poor handling until his turbocharger finally failed

84

Enforcement of skirt height at Zolder, using 6-cm measuring block. Lowering of hydraulic suspension systems in the race made entire regulation pointless

in the same class with that of the Williams. Nevertheless Ferrari was satisfied with its fairly strong debut, even if no points had been scored.

For the two races in South America in March and April the same three cars were taken but all had the KKK turbos and the Comprex system has not been used in a race, despite assurances of its continued development. The new sidepods with the smooth upper surfaces were mounted, these having small vertical louvres on the flanks. The Ferraris were disappointing in practice on the Jacarepagua circuit in Rio de Janeiro, Brazil; although 15-km/h (about 10-mph) faster on the straights than the Cosworth-powered cars, the Ferraris demonstrated such poor handling that Villeneuve did well to qualify seventh fastest and Pironi, after damaging his regular car, could only place the T-car (Training, or spare, chassis) seventeenth on the grid. The race was no more rewarding. Villeneuve's front and rear wings were bent in the scramble of the start, and although he was able to get up to sixth position before stopping to replace the front wing, his turbocharger failed at 25 laps. Pironi ran in mid-field until eliminated by a collision with the Renault turbo of Alain Prost.

The Comprex supercharger was tried again, briefly, in T-car 049 during practice for the Argentine Grand Prix in Buenos Aires, but its belt drive gave problems and he qualified twelfth using the KKK unit. Villeneuve, also with turbo power, was again seventh. The dismal South American showing was completed by two more retirements. Villeneuve demonstrated his admirable competitive spirit by fighting back to tenth place after spinning and dropping to twenty-second position on the first lap, but he spun again and retired with a broken driveshaft on lap 41. Pironi completed only three laps before his engine expired. Because of the amount of wing incidence the Ferraris had to employ to help their adhesion against rivals with better ground-effect chassis, they did not even enjoy the distinction of being fastest in a straight line.

Six retirements from six starts was not a very encouraging result from the first three races in the Americas, and Scuderia Ferrari returned to Europe and the serious task of implementing the modifications that were being tried constantly at Fiorano. The basic chassis was clearly inferior to those of the Williams, Brabham, Renault and perhaps several others, so there could be little expectation of a fully competitive car until a completely new monocoque and sidepods were designed. But if enthusiasts of the Italian team were discouraged, dreading another disastrous season like that of the 312 T5 in 1980, they needn't have been.

When the Ferrari turbos (050, 051 and a new car, 052) appeared next, at Imola for the San Marino Grand Prix in the middle of May, they were impressively fast. Several engine failures in practice cast doubts on the likelihood of the Ferrari turbos lasting the race, but the power was there—disgruntled rivals thought it to be in excess of 600 bhp with the boost turned way up for qualifying, and it was probably in the region of 545 bhp in race configuration. Villeneuve put the new chassis on the pole and Pironi was sixth best in 051. Chassis 050, with a spacer between the engine and gearbox extending the wheelbase by 125 mm (about 5 inches), was not raced even though Villeneuve liked its handling in practice a little better than the regular car.

For the first time since January 1980, when Villeneuve led the Brazilian Grand Prix for one demon lap in the 312 T5, Ferrari was at the front of the field. The two 126 CK turbos made the Italian crowd delirious by running one-two for fourteen laps, well clear of the other cars. Villeneuve had started on rain tires under the grey skies; it didn't rain so he came in for slicks as Piquet's hydraulically-suspended Brabham (the winner in Argentina) moved closer. The stop cost Gilles only 32 seconds and left Pironi in the lead, but then it *did* rain and Villeneuve had to stop for rain tires again, dropping to fourteenth place. This gave the Canadian the chance for an electrifying drive and the fastest lap, which he set at 1:48.064 on his forty-sixth; at the end of the race he was in seventh place.

Pironi held the lead until three-quarters distance, when a dislodged right skirt as well as diminished rear adhesion caused him to drop back to a fifth-place finish. The Ferraris had been the fastest cars at Imola and the turbo engines confounded the critics, and even suprised their drivers, by running strongly to the finish. Another problem, continuing the chaos that was becoming the rule for Formula 1, was making itself felt; the hydraulic suspension introduced by Brabham in South America was obviously against the regulations. But FISA allowed it as long as the cars could clear a 6-cm (approximately 2.4-inch) block when entering the pits. This meant that the cars with hydraulic suspension raced with the skirts (still rigid, as that part of the rule was not relaxed) right against the road, giving great adhesion but a rock-hard ride with almost no suspension travel, except to enter the pit lane. They were much faster than the conventionally-suspended cars, meaning that all the teams would have to follow suit. Most dissatisfied were the drivers, now placed in greater danger than ever before.

For Zolder in Belgium Ferrari took one standard car, 051, and two with hydraulically-adjustable suspension, numbers 059 and 052. Villeneuve, who more than any other driver liked a chassis he could fling about, ran 051 in practice until a driveshaft broke. He only got three laps in 050, not enough to improve on his time with the regular chassis, qualifying seventh. He admitted that the hydraulic suspension did give more downforce and would have to be used as long as the rules permitted it. Pironi, who ran all of practice with the system, was a satisfactory third after the qualifying sessions.

Making an excellent start, the French driver led the first twelve laps in his 126 CK. But as his handling deteriorated (the Ferrari was harder on the Michelins than any other chassis) he was only holding up the cars behind him, struggling to do so for as long as possible. He dropped down to fourth and eventually came in eighth as braking problems reduced his speed still further. Villeneuve had a race uncharacteristic of him, never challenging the leaders but driving steadily to a fourth-place finish. This was in no way a reflection of a less competitive temperament on this occasion, but rather the fact that his hydraulic suspension was jammed in the up position at the front. Perhaps truly characteristic of the great driver was his willingness to cope with an even more diabolic chassis than usual.

Gilles had not won a race since Watkins Glen in October 1979, enduring all of the 1980 season without complaint as the 312 T5 performed hopelessly and the 126 C continued its protracted development program. No driver ever tried to win more than Villeneuve—he

Opposite page *After trailing Jones for much of the Monte Carlo race, Villeneuve passed the Williams to take Ferrari's first turbo victory on 31 May 1981*

simply would not drive a car any slower than it could go—yet his patience was the mark of a mature driver, one who deserved to be a World Champion.

This patience was rewarded at Monte Carlo, and it was only fair that an element of luck should give him the long overdue victory. Although it had been rumoured that Ferrari would show up with an improved twin-Comprex system in Monaco, all four cars (050, 051 and 052, plus 049 which was brought quickly from Maranello when Pironi crashed the spare in practice) had KKK turbos. These were adjusted in what Ing. Forghieri called 'soft' form, with greater mid-range torque but less top-end power. This worked well and Villeneuve surprised everyone by placing a turbocharged car second on the grid on a tight street circuit. Pironi, however, had nothing but trouble in practice. After crashing 051 on Friday, he blew an engine in his race chassis (050) on Saturday and barely qualified (seventeenth among Monte Carlo's twenty starters) in 049 before crashing it as well. But his race performance would be just the opposite, a model of steadiness.

A water leak in the tunnel, from the efforts to put out a hotel fire above it, slowed all the cars at that point during the race. This was a particular disadvantage for Villeneuve, depriving him of speed at a place where his Ferrari had been fastest (yellow flags were displayed there throughout the race, forbidding any overtaking), so he was not able to match his qualifying pace. Nevertheless he ran in second or third position for 72 laps, despite gradually worsening brakes, and he was ready to pounce when the leading car, Jones' Williams, developed a misfire. Gilles swept past on lap 73, winning by forty seconds as the Williams stammered to the finish. And Pironi added to the Ferrari enthusiasts' delight by working his car up to fourth place as other machines dropped out.

The victory was Villeneuve's first in Europe and his fifth ever. It was certainly one of the most tiring, with the go-kart ride jarring his body and throwing his helmet against the rollbar. It was a popular win (Villeneuve lived in Monaco, and many of the spectators came from nearby Italy) and no one said he didn't deserve it, in spite of the fortunate circumstances. But no one expected another Ferrari victory at the next race in Spain.

At Jarama the fastest car was the Talbot Ligier-Matra V-12 of Jacques Laffite; the two Williams and the championship leader Reutemann were next, followed by the much-improved McLaren-Cosworth of John Watson and the Renault turbo of Prost. Even Bruno Giacomelli's Alfa Romeo qualified ahead of Villeneuve. But the Monte Carlo winner ran second to Jones for thirteen laps and took the lead the next time around. From then until the end of the race the Ferrari led a high-speed procession, with the better-handling cars trying to get by but never being able to make up for the turbo's power. It was a different kind of mastery that Villeneuve showed in Spain, one in which nerve and restraint were the main necessities. Pironi, who hit Patrese's Arrows at the start, had to stop on lap 20 to replace the damaged nose. Dropping to twenty-second position, he finally took fifteenth place, four laps behind.

Even with two victories back to back, Scuderia Ferrari did not think they had a championship contender on their hands. The 126 CK's

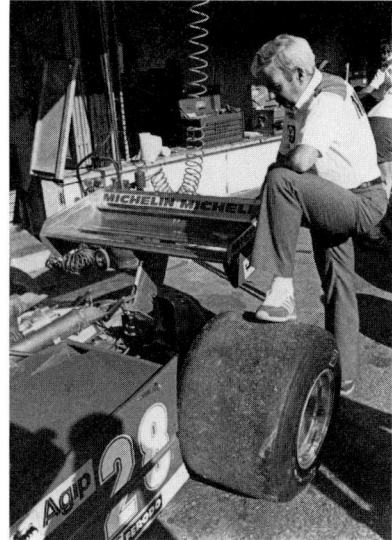

'Hmmm, may have to get one of those if they don't change the equivalency.' Teddy Mayer looks at 126 CK engine at Jarama

Opposite page *Villeneuve took second consecutive victory, leading a procession in Spain. Note two wheels off in lower photo*

89

'Hmmm, wish I had one of those in my Alfa.' Mario Andretti looks at 126 CK in Austria

engine progress had embarrassed (if only temporarily) the Renault team, which had three additional years of work in *its* turbo, but it was also apparent that Maranello's chassis was by far the worst among the competitive teams. Major improvements to the existing chassis were out of the question and an entirely new monocoque was called for.

Harvey Postlethwaite, the English designer of the successful Hesketh and Wolf Formula 1 cars, had recently resigned from the underfinanced Fittipaldi team. On June 7 he signed a contract with Ferrari, to assist Forghieri with chassis development on the 126 C. Structural and aerodynamic improvements were sorely needed; while only detail changes could be made to the existing layout for 1981, these would lead to an all-new car for 1982.

On the first weekend in July, at Dijon, the chassis 050, 052 and 053 appeared in long-wheelbase form, but otherwise little changed. The latter two machines qualified eleventh and fourteenth in the hands of Villeneuve and Pironi respectively, the worst showing for the team so far. Yet Villeneuve thrilled the crowd in the final practice session with his incredible car control, actually putting the 126 CK at a 90-degree angle to its direction of travel for over a hundred meters at 210 km/h (130 mph) *without* losing it. And this was after having crashed the same chassis at 225 km/h the day before. That his best practice lap should be so slow overall said a lot about the ground-effect of the other cars. (In retrospect this demonstration of bravery, so impressive at the the time, had a sad signficance.) Neither Ferrari went well in the French event, although Pironi took fifth place. Renault regained stature in front of its home crowd by taking pole position (René Arnoux) and winning the race (Prost's first Formula 1 victory).

At Silverstone two weeks later one 126 CK chassis, designated 051 B, appeared with a revised monocoque, reprofiled sidepods and new rear suspension geometry. This was still the work of Forghieri, as Postlethwaite had only been at Maranello for a month and a half, yet it had produced good results in testing at Hockenheim in Germany. Nevertheless both drivers used the standard layout in England (although chassis 053 and 054 did have new nose cones with full-width front wings mounted above, essentially the same arrangement that had been used on the flat-12 cars from 1974 through 1980). Pironi and Villeneuve ran second and third at the beginning of the race but retired early, with engine failure and front-end damage respectively. In Villeneuve's case, he at least did not persist in trying to get back to the pits in a heavily damaged car, as he had been criticized for doing in 1979 at Zandvoort. Watson's McLaren won the race after Arnoux's Renault failed eight laps from the finish; it was one of many occasions when that most unlucky French driver saw a well-deserved victory snatched from his grasp.

At Hockenheim, for the German Grand Prix, the Renaults dominated practice, having achieved top form in midseason. In contrast, the Ferrari challenge was fading, with Pironi and Villeneuve qualifying fifth and eighth. Again 051 B was brought along, now in long-wheelbase form, but it was used only in practice. Pironi completed only one lap of the race, in third position, before his engine expired, and Villeneuve also moved up two places during the opening laps. But he had to stop to change tires, falling to seventeenth and working hard to

Above *Ferrari's current team leader Didier Pironi*. Opposite page *the late Gilles Villeneuve, the most brilliant, hard-trying and sincere of Grand Prix drivers until his tragic death during final qualifying at Zolder in 1982*

91

Cockpit of 126 CK, with water temperature gauge high at right, oil/fuel pressure below it, 3–13,000-rpm tachometer in center and boost gauge at left (partly hidden in photo by steering wheel rim)

Opposite page *Front of 126 CK monocoque was revised in mid 1981; this photo can be compared with that of original design at the top of page 80*

126 CK engine in pits at Zandvoort, with exhaust pipes removed; note that the twin turbine impellers are spinning

Most competitive driver/car combination during 1981 was Nelson Piquet in the Brabham-Cosworth; he narrowly won World Championship in final race at Las Vegas

bring the Ferrari in tenth at the finish, one lap down on Piquet's winning Brabham.

At the Osterreichring the 126 CK raced in 'B' configuration for the first time, with the sidepods and rear suspension modified still further. The geometry at the back was essentially the same, but simpler rocker arms, not drilled out like the previous type, were employed. Villeneuve qualified third and charged into first place on the first lap. He had to take the escape road the next time around, rejoining in sixth place but crashing on lap twelve when he was in tenth position. Pironi started eighth and ran third at first but slipped down the field, one lap behind in ninth place at the finish. The performances showed that the Ferraris were always capable of challenging early in the races because of their engine power but generally unable to maintain the pace because of the mediocre chassis, which ate up tires if pushed hard. In Austria the winner was Laffite, whose Ligier outhandled the Renaults and swept past Arnoux fifteen laps from the end.

Scuderia Ferrari's fortune dropped to a season low in the Dutch Grand Prix at Zandvoort. Villeneuve qualified sixteenth in 050 B and didn't complete a lap, flying over Patrick Tambay's Ligier and Giacomelli's Alfa Romeo when trying to go between them, and ending up off the track in a shower of dirt after only 300 meters. Pironi did marginally better, qualifying 051 B in twelfth position and actually completing four laps before retiring with steering damage incurred in a separate collision with Tambay on lap one! The Ligier driver couldn't be blamed for either occurrence; he just happened to be there when the two frustrated Ferrari pilots tried to use all their turbo power to make up for the poor grid positions.

The team usually did better in Italy, with honor at stake in front of the home crowd. At Monza in September Pironi and Villeneuve worked no miracles but took the eighth and ninth starting spots in 049 B and 053 respectively. Gilles was more than a little annoyed by the fact that Didier used up three chassis in practice (crashing 054 on Friday and finding a bad vibration in 052 on Saturday), with the result that when Villeneuve blew an engine on Saturday his own spare T-car was not available and he could not improve on his time. In the race he went six laps before his turbocharger failed. On the other hand, Pironi went well, moving up to second place in the opening laps and eventually finishing fifth in a car that understeered because of ineffective skirts, a similar problem to that which had cost him a likely victory in the previous Italian event at Imola.

The Canadian Grand Prix at Montreal was a Michelin race because of the weather; the Goodyear runners were uncompetitive and the practice form was upset in the event itself. The two Ferraris had qualified only eleventh and twelfth but in the race the wet track suited their tires and Villeneuve got as high as second for a while, taking third place at the finish. Pironi ran as high as fourth but retired when his engine quit in lap 24.

There was a three-way fight for the World Championship title in the final race of 1981 at Las Vegas, but it did not involve either Ferrari driver. The circuit, laid out over the parking lot of the Caesar's Palace casino, was better than anyone had hoped; it was wider than expected and passing was possible. Villeneuve's fighting spirit earned him a

Hockenheim 1981: Gearbox, rear suspension and wing of 126 CK removes as a unit

Undertrays of 126 CK were in two halves; compare with one-piece design of 126 C2 as shown at the bottom of page 112

Opposite *Pironi running in mid-field at Monza; as scoring tower shows, leader was Prost (in Renault turbo number 15)*

third-place grid position and a brief second place in the race. Pironi's car was troubled by sticking skirts as well as turbo and fuel injection problems in practice and he could manage only eighteenth on the grid. He ran in mid-field for most of the race, taking ninth, two laps behind, at the flag. Villeneuve had already been disqualified for anticipating the start, but it made no difference (other than in the fact that the organizers were tardy in informing the team) as his engine stopped after twenty-two laps with fuel injection trouble, catching fire. None of the three title contenders (Carlos Reutemann, Nelson Piquet and Jacques Laffite) had a good race; it was Piquet's fifth-place finish which gave him a one-point margin over Reutemann in the final standings. Alan Jones, in his last race before retirement from Formula 1 competition, scored a runaway victory in the event.

Looking back on Ferrari's first full turbo season, one could see a satisfactory engine development program hampered by an ineffective chassis. The two victories had shown that Ferrari was always a threat, while the willingness of the two drivers to throw the ill-handling chassis about gave the spectators exciting moments. Some progress was made in chassis handling but it was more than offset by that among the other teams, Renault ending the year with the best combination of engine power and roadholding. During the year the Ferraris made thirty starts in the fifteen races, scoring two wins, one third place, two fourth places, three fifth places, one seventh, one eighth, two ninths, a tenth and a fifteenth. Villeneuve was seventh in the final World Championship order with 25 points and Pironi was thirteenth with 9. Of the sixteen retirements, five were the results of accidents, while the eleven mechanical failures can be summarized as follows: four engine internal, two turbocharger, two driveshaft, and one each fuel injection, electrical and oil leak.

In his first season with Scuderia Ferrari the performances of Pironi were usually almost as fast as those of Villeneuve, at least in practice, but the Canadian seemed to have a greater will to go fast, as well as better racecraft. It is a great tragedy that 1981 turned out to be Gilles' last full season.

Pages 98–99 *Villeneuve made good use of well-suited Michelins to take third place in Canadian Grand Prix. But note bent front wing, damaged earlier in race*

126 CK and CX Racing

Date	Circuit	Driver	Chassis	Qual.	Result
15/3/81	Long Beach (USA/W)	Villeneuve	126 CK 051	Q5	R, driveshaft
		Pironi	126 CK 050	Q11	R, fuel system
		(both)	126 CX 049	–	Practice only
29/3/81	Rio de Janeiro (BR)	Villeneuve	126 CK 051	Q7	R, turbo
		Pironi	126 CK 050	Q17	R, accident
		Pironi	126 CK 049	–	Practice only
12/4/81	Buenos Aires (RA)	Villeneuve	126 CK 051	Q7	R, driveshaft
		Pironi	126 CK 050	–	R, engine
		Pironi	126 CK 049	Q12	Practice only
3/5/81	Imola (SM)	Villeneuve	126 CK 052	Q1	7th and FL
		Pironi	126 CK 051	Q6	5th
		Villeneuve	126 CK 050	–	Practice only
17/5/81	Zolder (B)	Villeneuve	126 CK 050	–	4th
		Pironi	126 CK 052	Q3	8th
		Villeneuve	126 CK 051	Q7	Practice only
31/5/81	Monte Carlo (MC)	Villeneuve	126 CK 052	Q2	1st
		Pironi	126 CK 050	–	4th
		Pironi	126 CK 049	Q17	Practice only
		Pironi	126 CK 051	–	Practice only
21/6/81	Jarama (E)	Villeneuve	126 CK 052	Q7	1st
		Pironi	126 CK 053	Q13	15th
5/7/81	Dijon (F)	Villeneuve	126 CK 052	Q11	R, electrics
		Pironi	126 CK 053	Q14	5th
		Villeneuve	126 CK 050	–	Practice only
18/7/81	Silverstone (GB)	Villeneuve	126 CK 054	Q8	R, spin
		Pironi	126 CK 053	Q4	R, engine
		(both)	126 CK 051B	–	Practice only
2/8/81	Hockenheim (D)	Villeneuve	126 CK 054	Q8	10th
		Pironi	126 CK 053	Q5	R, engine
		Villeneuve	126 CK 051B	–	Practice only
16/8/81	Osterreichring (A)	Villeneuve	126 CK 051B	Q3	R, accident
		Pironi	126 CK 050B	Q8	9th
		Villeneuve	126 CK 054	–	Practice only
30/8/81	Zandvoort (NL)	Villeneuve	126 CK 050B	Q16	R, accident
		Pironi	126 CK 051B	Q12	R, accident
		Pironi	126 CK 054	–	Practice only

Performances 1981

Date	Circuit	Driver	Chassis	Qual.	Result
13/9/81	Monza (I)	Villeneuve	126 CK 053	Q9	R, turbo
		Pironi	126 CK 049B	Q8	5th
		Pironi	126 CK 052	–	Practice only
		Pironi	126 CK 054	–	Practice only
27/9/81	Montreal (CDN)	Villeneuve	126 CK 052	Q11	3rd
		Pironi	126 CK 049B	Q12	R, engine
		Villeneuve	126 CK 050B	–	Practice only
17/10/81	Las Vegas (USA)	Villeneuve	126 CK 052	Q3	R, fire
		Pironi	126 CK 049B	Q18	9th and FL
		Pironi	126 CK 051B	–	Practice only

Key: CK, KKK engine; CX, Comprex engine; B, revised monocoque; Q, qualifying position; R, retired; FL, fastest lap. Pole positions, victories and fastest laps indicated in **bold face**

Specifications—1981 126 CX and 126 CK

Engine: 120-degree V-6, mounted ahead of and driving rear wheels. Bore 81 mm, stroke 48.4 mm, displacement 1496.43 cm³ Gear-driven twin overhead camshafts for each bank of cylinders, operating two intake and two exhaust valves per cylinder. Comprex supercharger (CX) or KKK turbocharger (CK). Lucas fuel injection. Ignition by Marelli transistor. Single spark plug per cylinder. Compression ratio 6.5 :1. Power output 560 bhp at 11,500 rpm. Specific output 374.2 bhp/liter.

Transmission: Dry multi-plate clutch between engine and gearbox. 5 or 6-speed and reverse gearbox mounted transversely behind engine in unit with final drive.

Chassis: Aluminum monocoque. Fiberglass body panels. Side fairings giving aerodynamic downforce, with fixed skirts. Fuel tank capacity 210 liters (55.5 U.S. gallons).

Suspension: Hydraulic adjustment for ride height. Front, upper rocker arms, inboard coil spring/shock absorber units, wide-base lower A-arms, anti-roll bar. Rear, halfshafts with constant-velocity joints, upper rocker arms, inboard coil spring/shock absorber units, lower links, anti-roll bar. Brembo ventilated disc brakes, mounted out board front and rear. Center-lock Speedline cast magnesium-alloy 13-inch wheels with Michelin radial tires.

Dimensions: Wheelbase 2719-2850 mm (107.0–112.2 inches). Track 1700–1750 mm (66.9–68.9 inches) front, 1620 mm (63.8 inches) rear. Length 4468 mm (175.9 inches). Width 2099 mm (82.6 inches). Height, to rollbar, 1025 mm (40.3 inches). Weight, less fuel and driver, 610 kg (1345 pounds). Weight/power ratio 1.09 kg (2.40 pounds)/bhp.

Note: All figures potentially variable, especially those for track and width, dependent on wheels and tires mounted, and weight. Chassis numbers 049, 050, 051, 052, 053 and 054

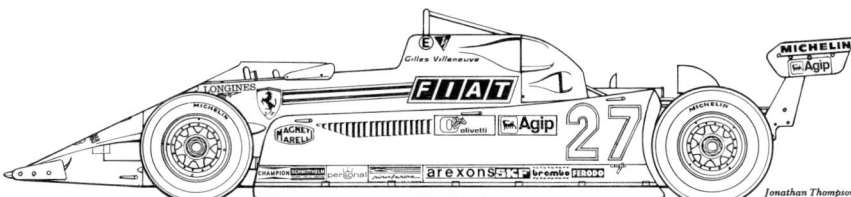

1981 126 CK as driven by Gilles Villeneuve at Monte Carlo (1/40 scale)

Chapter 5
the Postlethwaite-designed 126 C2

FERRARI BEGAN 1982 with an air of confidence that was well justified. The KKK-turbocharged engined had proved strong and surprisingly reliable very early in its first season, while the chassis deficiencies of the 1981 car were for the most part eliminated in the new design by Harvey Postlethwaite. Harvey, as most of the Italians chose to call him rather than tackle his difficult last name, had settled right in at his new job at Maranello. Although Mauro Forghieri's English was more than adequate for their direct consultations, Postlethwaite studied the Italian language as he studied Ferrari's handling problems. During the second half of 1981 his solutions were put on paper and construction of the resulting 126 C2 began in early winter.

When the new design made its first public appearance at the Ferrari press conference in the first week of the new year, it could be seen that the entire concept had been rethought. Expected to have a carbon-fiber monocoque, the 126 C2 used the material only for the front and rear bulkheads; the extremely narrow 'tub' was an aluminum/honeycomb structure, glued rather than riveted together. The car's total weight was thought to be close to the legal minimum of 580 kg (1278 pounds), compared to a high of 640 kg for the 126 CK in 1981. This reduction in weight was accompanied by an increase in engine output to 580 bhp at race boost (for qualifying over 600 bhp could be used). The engine was still KKK-turbocharged, although it was claimed at the press showing that work was continuing on the Comprex supercharger, and that still another type of boost system had already been tested on Maranello's dynometers! But at the time of writing, mid-1982, no evidence had been seen that either program was about to result in a new engine for actual racing.

Slightly revised, the gearbox was still a transverse unit, although again it was stated that a new, longitudinal, transmission had been designed for the appearance in mid-season. The suspension was modified at both ends, and particular attention was given to making clean tunnels at the back of the sidepods, with inner paneling sweeping up over the rear driveshafts. In contrast to the 126 CK, on which the paneling was made in two halves, the 126 C2 had a one-piece undertray which fit around the narrow monocoque and extended out to the flanks.

The bodywork was not drastically changed in appearance, but initially the front suspension fairings were angled airfoils and the upper surfaces of the main pods were curved at the sides (this latter

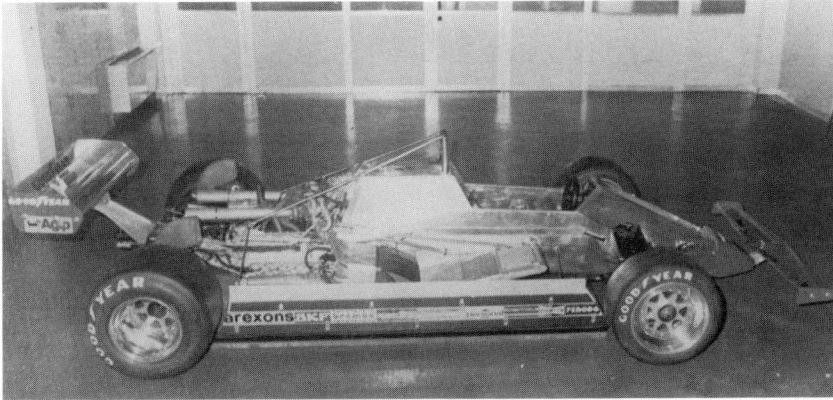

Harvey Postlethwaite's 126 C2 was presented to the press at Fiorano in January 1982. Much tidier monocoque made only minimal use of carbon-fiber material but weight was significantly reduced. Front wing was mounted above nose at first; later there were two planes at sides of nose, or none, depending on the circuit. Ground-effect air was tunneled through rear suspension much more effectively

Pironi tests 126 C2 at Fiorano before first race at Kyalami. Other tests were conducted at Paul Ricard circuit in France

Cowling of 126 C2 comes off in one piece. Front suspension fairings were later blended into upper surfaces and, still later, almost eliminated. This photo was taken during initial testing at Paul Ricard in January

106

change had also been made to revised examples of the 126 CK then being tested). A front wing was mounted on the car shown to the press; it use depended on the varying demands of the different circuits. Without the wing, in testing and in several early races, the 126 C2 looked quite different, cleaner and more aggressive than it predecessor. As was the factory's usual practice at press showings, each side of the car carried a different name and number, 'Gilles/27' on the right and 'Didier/28' on the left.

The name Goodyear appeared on Ferrari bodywork again after a four-year absence during which the team had a tire contract with Michelin. The 126 C2 was immediately fast in testing, Villeneuve shattering the Fiorano track record, while over 800 kilometers (approximately 500 miles) of proving runs were completed at Paul Ricard without any engine trouble whatsoever. As did most of the Formula 1 teams, Ferrari went to South Africa in advance of the Kyalami even in order to log some serious comparative runs. In the pre-race testing, Villeneuve's 1:06.65 was third best, just about a second slower than Prost's fastest run with the Renault RE 30B, while Pironi was another second slower in the other 126 C2 at 1:07.59.

As has almost come to be the norm for Formula 1 races, the Kyalami event on the third weekend in January saw another political squabble, this one a driver protest over fines and other conditions imposed by FISA for their alleged transgressions in the past. A race-day strike was avoided, but not before serious doubts had been raised about the likelihood of a start, some of the teams even pretending that they would employ inexperienced drivers rather than support their regular members against FISA. Practice times put the extremely earnest René Arnoux on the pole in his RE 30B, but the Ferrari of Villeneuve split the Renaults on the grid, as did the new BMW turbo-powered Brabhams, appearing with the German four-cylinder 1.5-liter engines for the first time. Pironi, qualifying behind Prost, completed the sextet of turbocharged cars at the front. The fact that Kyalami's high altitude favored boosted induction was shown by the mid-field qualification of Derek Warwick's Toleman-Hart turbo, a car that had seldom even qualified in 1981, and then only at the very back of the grid. This made seven turbos in the race, the most that had started so far but still less than one-third of the field.

The race was a runaway for the two Renaults, with Prost the ultimate winner even after a pit stop to replace a punctured tire, but the two Ferraris ran strongly in third and fourth positions for six laps. Villeneuve's turbo failed at that point, Pironi taking over third for eighteen more laps before having to stop for tires himself. He worked back up to second by lap 61 but dropped to the end of the field with a misfiring engine, eventually being classified as a finisher in eighteenth position, six laps behind. Nevertheless the Ferrari 126 C2s had made a promising debut, with a vast improvement in handling that made them competitive until let down by uncharacteristic engine troubles.

As the political battles raged on, with FISA president Jean-Marie Balestre now siding with FOCA against the so-called 'Grandee' manufacturers' teams (Ferrari, Renault and Alfa Romeo), it was apparent that rules meant nothing and that interpretation was wide, according to the intentions and relative competitiveness of each team.

In general, the FOCA teams, mostly using the venerable Ford Cosworth V-8 engine, opposed turbocharging on general principle, wishing to change the equivalence to 1.4 liters to make them less potent (this also included Brabham, run by the FOCA boss Bernie Ecclestone, who was more than willing to scrap his BMW turbo program in order to retain commercial control of the overall Formula 1 scene). Having already won a battle over their interpretation of the skirt and ground-clearance rule in 1981, the FOCA members had another 'fifth ace' up their sleeves. This was an on-board water reservoir, ostensibly to cool the brakes but in fact a disposible volume that reduced the total car weight below the legal minimum at the conclusion of the race. This was an effective though blatantly illegal weapon against the turbocharged cars, which were generally heavier to begin with and not likely to get below the minimum, not even counting the extra weight of fuel that their thirstier engines required. The turbo teams (including Alfa Romeo, with its unraced 1.5-liter V-8 still under development) argued, quite correctly, that the turbo equivalence had been established in the past and that its opponents did not have the right to break the rules simply because the turbos had finally become competitive.

The Renault of Prost and the Ferrari of Villeneuve qualified at the front of the pack for the Brazilian Grand Prix at the Rio Autodrome in March, but it was the local hero and reigning World Champion Nelson Piquet who won in his Brabham, Cosworth-powered again and running with the controversial water tank, as was the second-place Williams-Cosworth of Keke Rosberg. Villeneuve gave the 126 C2 its most promising showing yet by leading the race for twenty-nine laps, in front of the two Renaults and Piquet, finally succumbing to the relentless pressure of the Brazilian driver and spinning off, out of the race. Pironi, who started eighth in the other Ferrari, spun on lap three, dropping from sixth to sixteenth place; he worked up to ninth position, pitted for new tires without losing a place, and eventually finished eighth. After the race Gilles admitted that he simply could not keep the Ferrari on the road at the pace being forced by Piquet. The Postlethwaite-designed 126 C2 was much superior to the 1981 car in roadholding but still deficient in this respect to the best of the English cars, notably the Williams, Brabham, McLaren and Tyrrell, as well as the Renault. In order not to sacrifice straightaway speed, as had been clearly necessary in Brazil the year before, the Ferraris were still running without front wings at Rio.

At Long Beach for the United States Grand Prix West the first week in April, the Ferraris had front wings (mounted on the sides of the nose-cone rather than above it as on the press preview car) as well as a novel twin rear wing. Because there was a rule limiting the width of the rear wing, Ferrari chose to employ two separate planes, with a total width extending to the outer edges of the rear tires, stating that there was no rule on the *number* of rear airfoils. This was true, as several teams had run biplane wings of legal width, but Ferrari's interpretation could be seen as more of a challenge to the similar rule-bending of the water-tank cars than as a technical improvement. But the tight Long Beach street circuit did require more downforce than straight-line speed, and Villeneuve did start the race, fifth on the grid, with the controversial, almost humorously provocative device. Another change seen for this

Villeneuve and Pironi ran third and fourth behind Renaults in 126 C2 debut at Kyalami

This photo, taken at Kyalami, shows well the routing of charged air through intercoolers at each side of chassis, then to induction 'log' below each cylinder bank

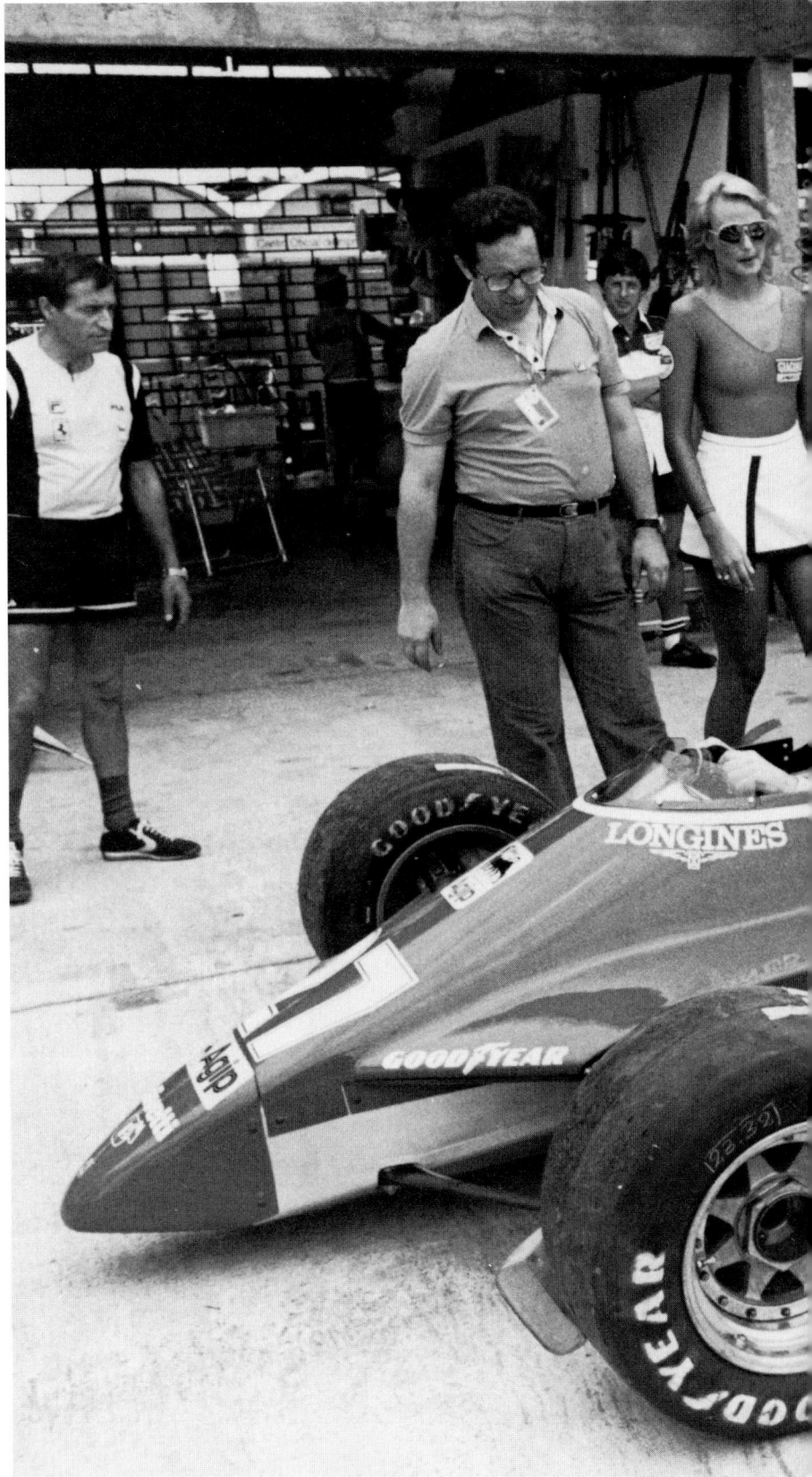

Forghieri and Villeneuve in discussion at Rio, seemingly unaware of Giacobazzi public relations operations in the foreground. Note simplicity of 126 C2 nose without front wing

event was the blending of the front suspension fairings into the upper bodywork. Pironi qualified his Ferrari tenth, two-fifths of a second slower than Villeneuve. By this time there were five 126 C2 chassis in existence, number 055 through 059, with the first three being taken to Long Beach. (Seven 126 C chassis had been built during 1980–1981.)

Gilles turned in a strong performance in the race (which resulted in the first victory for Niki Lauda since he had returned to Formula 1 as a member of the McLaren team); the fighting Canadian battled with Rosberg's Williams for many laps and eventually took third place on a circuit not at all suited to his Ferrari. He even overshot Turn 1 on one occasion, braking late in an attempt to pass Rosberg and half-spinning as he saw he couldn't make it; pointed the right way as his car came to a halt, he was able to get going again before Piquet arrived and thus did not lose a place. But he did lose the place when the regulations were imposed after the race, finding his rear wing illegal and disqualifying him. Pironi started ninth and ran briefly in sixth position before sliding into a wall on the sixth lap; this was the fate of many cars as a result of a poorly-cured road surface.

The question of water tanks was finally resolved by a belated FISA decision in mid-April disqualifying Piquet and Rosberg from their first and second finishing positions at Rio, elevating Prost to winner of that race and all the other finishers two places higher. This so enraged the FOCA teams that they boycotted the Imola race on April 25. As it was likely that most of their members were by then running underweight cars that could not have passed a post-race weighing, this was more an admission of non-compliance than of indignation (of the fourteen cars that did run—two each Renault, Ferrari, Tyrrell, Alfa Romeo, Osella, Toleman and ATS—only the Italian-sponsored Tyrrell was a usual FOCA supporter, while the non-FOCA Alfa Romeo team had to add ballast to its cars to meet the minimum figure). Niki Lauda showed stature by appearing at the event, as a matter of principle, even though the McLaren team did not. With so few runners, it was rumored that a third Ferrari would be made available to the unemployed driver, but in fact this was not really possible because of contractual obligations.

The absence of the FOCA teams probably had little effect on the outcome of the Imola race (run as the San Marino Grand Prix) and it certainly did not diminish the pleasure of the Italian crowd, which saw the Ferrari team take its first one-two finish since 1979. Qualifying third and fourth behind the two Renaults, Villeneuve and Pironi outlasted the French cars and ran close together for the second half of the race, exchanging positions to the delight of the spectators. Villeneuve, as the leader when the Renaults expired, assumed that team rules would guarantee his victory and that Pironi would behave on the last lap and drop behind him; more important, he realized that both Ferraris could run out of fuel if Pironi continued to force the pace. He was more than annoyed when Didier did race past him on the last lap and take the victory. It was the first win for the French driver since he joined Ferrari; much as the crowd loved the 'duel,' Enzo Ferrari later came out in support of Gilles, if not exactly chastizing Didier for snatching the victory. The pit signals *had* said 'Slow' when Villeneuve was ahead, as the fuel situation was a close thing. In addition to his win, Pironi took the fastest lap at 1:35.036.

Although taken at separate races (Rio and Long Beach), these two photos give good indications of the bare chassis and of the one-piece undertray with upswept panels at each side. Note how narrow the actual monocoque is compared to sidepod width

113

The Imola incident caused a rift between the two previously friendly Ferrari drivers, one which, tragically, was never patched up. Less than two weeks later, on May 8, 1982, Gilles Villeneuve was killed on his final qualifying lap during the final practice session for the Belgian Grand Prix at Zolder. Trying with everything he had to improve his time—at that point good for a seventh starting position—Gilles was launched into the air when he ran over the right rear tire of Jochen Mass's March-Cosworth as he tried to pass the slower car. Although he was not pronounced dead until later at the hospital, he was in effect killed instantly when his car came down nose first at 150 mph, disintegrating and throwing him out as it hit. Some criticism was voiced over the fact that his seatbelts were torn out by the impact, rather than keeping him inside the monocoque, but this can have made no difference to his fate. An examination of the wreck later showed that the impact had caused the belt mounts to be sheared off from the monocoque and that the belts themselves had not broken. Almost everyone at the track realized Gilles had been lost even before the announcement came from the hospital. Understandably, the Ferrari team withdrew the other car from the race and returned to Italy in a despondency that was felt by the entire world of racing. The following day's race was won by John Watson's McLaren; true to form, there was yet another disqualification, Lauda's similar car being 2 kg light.

Although Villeneuve was a Canadian and resided in Monaco, he was the greatest favorite of the Italian public, which expressed its grief in every imaginable way, from wreaths laid outside the Fiorano track and the dedication of a street to his name, to the painting of a Canadian flag on his starting position at Imola. The rest of the world followed suit, with the Montreal circuit being renamed for him and the 1983 Dutch Grand Prix at Zandvoort being designated as a memorial event. Aside from his great skill as a driver and his absolute dedication to going as fast as possible even when a victory was impossible, Gilles Villeneuve was a man who stood at the top of his profession. He was sincere and considerate at all times, never offering excuses or taking the cheap, self-serving path. He acknowledged his mistakes—at the speeds he drove he had to make them sometimes—and never shied from his responsibilities. Most of all he was a true sportsman who loved his work and had the greatest respect for the most important element of all, the public which paid to see him perform. He always gave them their money's worth.

Beyond the loss of Villeneuve, the sport of motor racing in general and that of Formula 1 in particular must come to grips with a number of crucial problems. The question of safety must be resolved by the abolition of the ground-effect technology which actually gives a less satisfying spectacle at the same time that it places drivers in ever greater jeopardy. The same is true of qualifying tires. And while it is realized that almost all modern sports are in fact big business, that business is the entertainment of the paying public. All technicalities aside, no business can afford to disregard its patrons' sensibilities repeatedly. The inevitable lawyers in motor racing must establish logical rules that maintain the spirit of competition. Then they must maintain the integrity of what has been agreed upon and let the drivers get on with the racing.

Perhaps as much a slap at the sorry state of the Formula 1 regulations as it was a technical solution, Ferrari's two-plane rear wing (opposite page, top) was disqualified after Long Beach race. Villeneuve, battling with Keke Rosberg in the lower photo, lost his hard-earned points

115

In a continuing attempt to get more rear adhesion, this two-plane wing (of legal width!) was tried in practice at Imola

In Imola race, boycotted by most FOCA teams, Arnoux's Renault led initially, followed here by Pironi's 126 C2

Pages 118–119 After Renaults failed, the Imola race was a two-way fight between Ferraris of Villeneuve and Pironi. The Canadian obeyed the team's SLOW signal (important because fuel was marginal for the distance) but Pironi, eager for his first Ferrari victory, drove all-out and took the finish ahead of his team-mate. Note that Pironi ran with a front wing, Villeneuve without

126 C2 Racing Performances to June 1982

Date	Circuit	Driver	Chassis	Qual.	Result
23/1/82	*Kyalami*	*Villeneuve*	*126 C2 055*	*Q3*	*R, turbo*
	(ZA)	*Pironi*	*126 C2 056*	*Q6*	*18th*
21/3/82	*Rio de Janeiro*	*Villeneuve*	*126 C2 057*	*Q2*	*R, accident*
	(BR)	*Pironi*	*126 C2 056*	*Q8*	*6th**
4/4/82	*Long Beach*	*Villeneuve*	*126 C2 058*	*Q7*	*Disqualified***
	(USA/W)	*Pironi*	*126 C2 056*	*Q9*	*R, accident*
		Villeneuve	*126 C2 057*	*–*	*Practice only*
25/4/82	*Imola*	*Villeneuve*	*126 C2 058*	*Q3*	*2nd*
	(SM)	*Pironi*	*126 C2 059*	*Q4*	**1st and FL**
		Pironi	*126 C2 057*	*–*	*Practice only*
9/5/82	*Zolder*	*Villeneuve*	*126 C2 058*	*(Q8)*	*Fatal accident in practice*
	(B)	*Pironi*	*126 C2 059*	*(Q6)*	*Entry withdrawn*
		Pironi	*126 C2 057*	*–*	*Practice only*
23/5/82	*Monte Carlo*	*Pironi*	*126 C2 059*	*Q5*	*2nd*
	(MC)	*Pironi*	*126 C2 057*	*–*	*Practice only*
6/6/82	*Detroit*	*Pironi*	*126 C2 057*	*Q4*	*3rd*
	(USA)	*Pironi*	*126 C2 059*	*–*	*Practice only*
13/6/82	*Montreal*	*Pironi*	*126 C2 059*	*–*	*9th and* **FL**
	(CDN)	*Pironi*	*126 C2 057*	*Q1*	*Damaged in first start*

Key: *Q, qualifying position; R, retired; FL, fastest lap; *Finished 8th but classified 6th after first two disqualified; **Finished 3rd but excluded for illegal rear wing. Pole positions, victories and fastest laps indicated in* **boldface**

Specifications—1982 126 C2

Engine: *120-degree V-6, mounted ahead of and driving rear wheels. Bore 81 mm, stroke 48.4 mm, displacement 1496.43 cm³. Gear-driven twin overhead camshafts for each bank of cylinders, operating two intake and two exhaust valves per cylinder. KKK turbocharger. Lucas fuel injection. Ignition by Marelli transistor. Single spark plug per cylinder. Compression ratio 6.5:1. Power output 580 bhp at 11,000 rpm. Specific output 387.5 bhp/liter.*

Transmission: *Dry multi-plate clutch between engine and gearbox. 5 or 6-speed and reverse gearbox mounted transversely or longitudinally behind engine in unit with final drive.*

Chassis: *Aluminum/honeycomb bonded monocoque with carbon-fiber bulkheads. Fiberglass body panels. Side fairings giving aerodynamic downforce, with fixed skirts. Fuel tank capacity 210 liters (55.5 U.S. gallons).*

Suspension: *Hydraulic adjustment for ride height. Front, upper rocker arms, inboard coil spring/shock absorber units, wide-base lower A-arms, anti-roll bar. Rear, halfshafts with constant-velocity joints, upper rocker arms, inboard coil spring/shock absorber units, lower links, anti-roll bar. Brembo ventilated disc brakes, mounted outboard front and rear. Center-lock cast magnesium-alloy 13-inch and 15-inch wheels with Goodyear tires.*

Dimensions: *Wheelbase 2657.8–2856 mm (104.6–112.8 inches). Track 1787.4 mm (70.4 inches) front, 1644 mm (64.7 inches) rear. Length 4333 mm (170.6 inches), width 2110 mm (83.1 inches). Height, to rollbar, 1025 mm (40.3). Weight, less fuel and driver, 595 kg (1312 pounds). Weight/power ratio 1.025 kg (2.26 pounds)/bhp.*

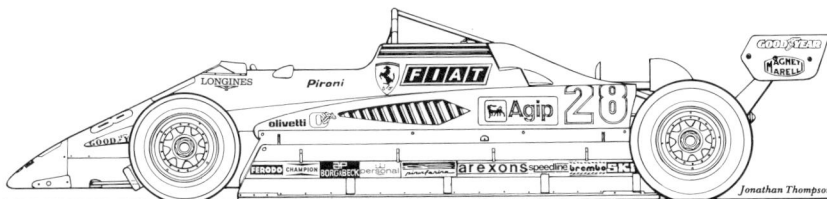

1982 126 C2 as driven by Didier Pironi at Imola (1/40 scale)

Chapter 6
Prototype and GT turbos

AS IN ROAD RACING, it was Porsche that brought turbochargers to the production Grand Touring car. The purpose, of course, was for increased power. But the worldwide concentration on reduced exhaust emissions and improved fuel economy made the turbo an attractive— though initially expensive—proposition for more prosaic road machinery, and by the mid-Seventies even the lowly Diesel sedan could make effective use of boosted induction. Ferrari, on the other hand, had always been slow to adopt technology pioneered by other firms, taking a 'wait and see if it's really here to stay' attitude. This had been true of the disc brake and the rear-mounted engine; in racing, Ferrari was one of the last to adopt the monocoque chassis in the mid-Sixties and the skirted ground-effect chassis in the late-Seventies.

Ferrari's production GT cars, though reasonably powerful (in their European versions, at least), have been characterized by a robust construction, with excessive weights that have robbed them of the acceleration one expects from an expensive, exotic sports machine. The problem was even greater on the American market, where strict anti-pollution requirements reduced the power output to the point that acceleration lagged behind that of far more ordinary machinery costing a third as much. In the case of the 308 GTB and GTS, the 3-liter V-8's initial output of 255 bhp was reduced to only 205 bhp, even on the latest fuel-injected versions. Turbo boost was clearly called for.

While the factory took its time in this area, private enthusiasts set about solving the problem with the equipment at hand. The engineering expense of converting the 308 to turbo induction was such that few individuals could afford to pour it all into a single car, so the solution was the specialist-manufactured turbocharger kit, with all the necessary hardware for the conversion. This approach had the advantage of applying the turbo manufacter's emissions test results to the certification of all the cars so modified. The two major U.S. manufacturers of turbocharger kits for Ferraris have been BAE in Torrance, California and Ameritech in Danbury, Connecticut, while Janspeed of Salisbury has produced conversion kits for the English market.

BAE, already experienced in manufacturing a wide variety of turbo kits for other cars, has been the most prominent in the area of Ferrari conversions, with approximately 250 turbo kits having been sold between 1980 and the time of writing. Costing $3500 with wastegate and full exhaust system, or $3700 if a catalytic converter is supplied,

Carma FF 308 GTB/4 Biturbo ran in seven 1981 events, including Daytona (left), Mugello (center) and Silverstone (bottom); though extremely fast, it never lasted

Pages 124–125 Facetti's Biturbo belches flame during practice at Silverstone

the BAE system does not guarantee a specific power output but rather a 50-percent increase in power at the rear wheels, this of course being dependent upon the performance of the original engine and drivetrain. BAE had found that boosts ranging between 3.5 and 7 pounds were appropriate for road car conversions; on the 308 it is 5.5, resulting in approximately 245 bhp at the wheels on most examples. (Using normally unobtainable 108-Octaine fuel and a 9-pound boost, 300 bhp was seen on one test 308.) BAE kits are installed by any authorized Ferrari dealer and certain other BAE outlets; along with the conversion comes a certification that the system has met Federal emissions requirements.

The author drove a BAE-equipped 308 GTBi early in 1982. From the outside there was no indication that the car was turbocharged, although the owner can mount a chromium 'Turbo' script on the rear, or use BAE's decal if desiring to broadcast the conversion. Similarly, because of the 308's tight transverse installation, the BAE system does not markedly change the appearance of the engine compartment. The sound is different, of course, when the engine is fully wound out, but by then the driver of any nearby car will be aware that he has met with more than a standard 308. The first two seconds off the line are not shattering, but the turbo engine gets quickly into its stride and the power continues right up to 6000 rpm. The feeling is like that in one of the lightest European-spec 308 GTBs, restoring the car to the kind of performance that its aggressive appearance calls for and its superior handling and braking are equipped to deal with. Test figures recorded by *Motor Trend* magazine, admittedly with a prime example prepared especially by BAE, are as follows:

	Stock	BAE Turbo
0–30 mph	2.5 seconds	2.2 seconds
0–40 mph	3.8	3.1
0–50 mph	5.5	4.8
0–60 mph	7.9	6.0
Standing-start quarter-mile	15.9	14.3
Speed at end	88 mph	95 mph

The author also had the opportunity to examine, but not drive, a one-of-a-kind BB 512 turbocharged by BAE's Bob McClure for his personal use, This fantastic machine had a mechanical beauty to match its performance, including a power output of 600 bhp (estimated) and a maximum speed of over 200 mph. Not having to meet the daily demands that might be placed on a marketed system by an insensitive owner, the BB 512 had a revised fuel injection system and twin Rayjay turbos running at a 10-pound boost, producing nearly incredible power right up to 8000 rpm. Moving off the line at 3000 rpm, McClure's BB achieved a quarter-mile time of 13.2 seconds and 121 mph in a test conducted by Fred Gregory for *Motor Trend*. McClure claimed to have reached 7800 rpm in fifth gear in his Boxer, which works out to just about 200 mph; one wonders what road was used!

Another less documented BB 512 converted to turbo power as well as to open Targa-type configuration was a Trend Engineering project in 1980. Trend's Al Mardikian did not give a horsepower figure, but a

Special turbocharged BB, built by Jean-Louis Château in 1977, never competed. Note similarity of nose to Porsche 917

127

Pages 128–129 Trend turbocharged BB 512 was also converted into Targa-style spyder

brief run by *Road Test* magazine produced a quarter-mile speed of 111 mph. Similar conversions, including the Targa roof, would be quoted in excess of $130,000 if undertaken by Trend.

The Ameritech turbo conversion for the 308, costing $6400 and consisting of 114 custom-engineered components, also uses the Rajay turbine and wastegate, in conjunction with a Carter AFB 9400 AF carburetor. Ameritech's Dick Fritz quotes considerably more power than BAE, with maximums at 6 psi of 320–330 bhp and 305 lb-ft torque. Air filter, manifolding, exhaust pipes and muffler are all manufactured especially for the 308 by Ameritech and the underhood appearance of the red-painted components is impressive. Tested by *Autoweek* this turbo system produced a 0–60 time of 4.8 seconds and a quarter-mile speed of 108 mph on a coveted 308 GTS. *Car and Driver* recorded figures of 5.7 seconds and 102 mph, respectively. But it is a conversion intended for track use and is not certified for the highway, carrying a sticker saying 'For Offroad Use Only'.

More modest, Janspeed's turbo conversion employs a Garrett blower at 5.25 psi to add approximately 30–40 bhp to the 230 or so produced by the European version of the 308 in stock form. At a cost of £4500 (on a version of the car already producing reasonable power) this could be a questionable modification, and *Car* magazine found the system suffered from some shortcomings in driveability and aesthetics, though producing effortless power and a maximum speed of 165 mph in fifth gear.

Very few turbocharged Prototype racing Ferraris have been produced. Built but never raced was a well-documented BB 512 modified by Jean-Louis Château for the 1977 Le Mans 24-hour event. Called the 512 Turbo GTP, it was reputed to have 520 bhp, not an impressive output for a Prototype. Also heavily modified was the bodywork, but the project was abandoned after Château found that the standard Boxer lubrication system was not up to the task.

Actually raced for a full season of Group 5 events in 1981 was the Carma FF 308 GTB4 Biturbo. In addition to twin Garrett blowers, the 3-liter engine had 32-valve cylinder heads and one can speculate on the amount of technical cooperation extended by the Ferrari factory. Power output was a nearly-unmanageable (considering the car's braking capability) 830–840 bhp for qualifying and approximately 750 bhp in race form. Even the later figure could not be produced reliably without early failures, but the car was a phenomenal performer while it lasted. Although the bodywork was extensively modified in the current Group 5 mode, the original Ferrari chassis was retained, resulting in a race weight of 1030 kg (2270 pounds).

Driven by Carlo Facetti and Martino Finotto (whose names provided the basis for the team name), the Carma FF 308 GTB4 Biturbo contested the Daytona, Mugello, Monza Silverstone, Nürburgring, Enna and Kyalami events; most were 1000-km (621-mile) or 6-hour events, although Daytona was for 24 hours and Kyalami a 9-hour race. In any case, the car did not complete the full distance of even the shorter events, nevertheless being good for spectator entertainment in the early laps! At Daytona the car set the fastest lap at 1 : 48.14 (205.568 km/h or 127.658 mph) when in second place, before breaking down on the fourth lap with electrical and cooling troubles. Starting sixth at

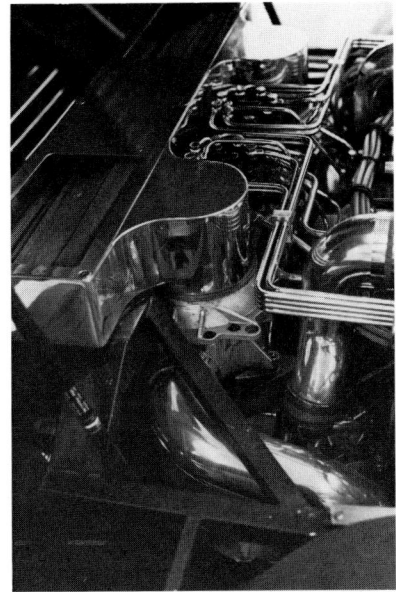

Twin Rajay turbos of McClure's BB 512 lurked at rear of engine compartment

131

Opposite Most potent BB of all was 512 converted to twin turbos by Bob McClure of BAE. Note extremely fine detail finish

Mugello, Facetti brought the car up to second by the first turn but touched Michele Alboreto's Lancia and dropped to third; the engine failed at twenty laps. At Monza the Carma FF qualified for the pole, reaching over 200 mph on the long straight, but broke a turbo on the warm-up lap and did not start. At Silverstone the car lost fifth gear during practice and it eventually qualified sixth (second in the Group 5 class) at 1:24.88, using a 750-bhp race engine along with a new gearbox. It was plagued by various troubles on the race, retiring at half-distance.

If the Nürburgring was considered too dangerous for 500-bhp Formula 1 cars, one can imagine the difficulty in getting the Carma FF Biturbo around the circuit. Bravery was essential, but not enough. Facetti lost the car at the Flugplatz, damaging it to the extent that it could not be made ready for the race. The car qualified on the pole at Enna with a time of 1:36.08, leading at the start (it was the only Group 5 car entered) but retiring in flames on the third lap. In its final 1981 appearance at Kyalami the car blew up spectacularly at the two-hour point when running in sixth place. Despite the unquestioned speed of the Carma FF Biturbo it was too difficult to drive and too complicated a project for the small team; although the car was made ready for 1982 competition, its drivers concentrated on more-raceable Porsche equipment.

Considering the publicity achieved by the Carma project, as well as the demand for more power on the part of regular 308 GTB and GTS owners, the first production Ferrari turbo was a long time coming. Having used KKK turbochargers in Formula 1, Ferrari employed the German firm's equipment for its production car project, but not without testing other systems including the American BAE unit. Turbo 308s in both berlinetta and spyder body styles circulated the Fiorano test track throughout 1981, these being identifiable by the additional NACA-type scoops ahead of each rear wheel (the GTB also had a Boxer-style airfoil above the rear deck). It was rumored that both 2-liter and 3-liter turbo versions of the V-8 engine were under test, the former for the European market and the latter for American customers.

The 2-liter car was finally announced in May 1982, appearing at the Torino Salone as the Ferrari 208 GTB and GTS Turbo. The 1991-cc unit was KKK-boosted, as expected, with a quoted output of 220 bhp at 7000 rpm (compared to the larger 308 GTBi's 214 bhp at 6600). Even without an intercooler, the turbocharged V-8 was a tight fit. One example, a red car with '208 Turbo' in large yellow lettering on each side, was displayed next to the Scuderia Ferrari transporter in the pits at Imola, where the Formula 1 team gave the crowd a rousing one-two victory. The Ferrari turbo era had truly arrived.

While the 208 Turbo has a greater output than the normally-aspirated 3-liter V-8, there has been further speculation about a 308 Turbo, from which a power output of 320 bhp might be projected. This would go a long way in making Ferrari more competitive with Porsche in the high-performance production GT market, but factory sources give more weight to a 32-valve unturbocharged 308 for the American market. In any case, Ferrari development continues at its always prolific rate.

Opposite page *Ferrari factory finally entered the turbo market with the 208 Turbo, presented at Torino show in GTB form. Aileron on roof and NACA-type scoops in rocker panels were main external identifying features. KKK-boosted 2-liter engine produced 220 bhp at 7000 rpm; torque was a healthy 24.5 kg/m (177 lb/ft) at 4800 rpm. Maximum speed was quoted at 242 km/h (right on 150 mph) and fuel consumption at 13 liters/100 km (approximately 18 mpg)*

133

Pages 134–135 *Pininfarina press photo of 208 Turbo. First example was silver*

Acknowledgements

Photographs

*Alfa Romeo SpA / Vincente Alvarez /
John Blakemore / Jeff Bloxham /
Peter Coltrin / Steve Dawson / Art Flores /
Guy Griffiths / Jeff Hutchinson /
Ed Ikuta / Bernard Lemeunier /
Jean François Marchet / Corrado
Millanta / Phipps Photographic /
Industrie Pininfarina /
Publifoto / Renault Presse /
Alessandro Stefanini / Jonathan
Thompson / Bob Tronolone /
Renardo Volpe / Kurt Wörner*

Drawings

*Ferrari SEFAC / R. Ingrani /
Renault Presse / Jonathan Thompson*

*Additional information was provided by
Dick Fritz of Ameritech, Gary Jacobs of
BAE, Richard Jordan, Tom Kowaleski of
Renault USA Inc., Otis Meyer of* Road &
Track *and Sergio Montorsi of Fiat
Motors of North America.*